WORLDCOMP'13
July 22-25, 2013
Las Vegas Nevada, USA
www.world-academy-of-science.org

PROCEEDINGS OF THE 2013 INTERNATIONAL CONFERENCE ON COMPUTER GRAPHICS & VIRTUAL REALITY

CGVR 2013

Editors

Hamid R. Arabnia
Leonidas Deligiannidis
Ashu M. G. Solo

FIREWALL MEDIA
(An Imprint of Laxmi Publications Pvt. Ltd.)
An ISO 9001:2008 Company

BENGALURU • CHENNAI • COCHIN • GUWAHATI • HYDERABAD
JALANDHAR • KOLKATA • LUCKNOW • MUMBAI • RANCHI • NEW DELHI
BOSTON (USA) • ACCRA (GHANA) • NAIROBI (KENYA)

This volume contains papers presented at The 2013 International Conference on Computer Graphics & Virtual Reality (CGVR'13). Their inclusion in this publication does not necessarily constitute endorsements by editors or by the publisher.

Branches

Bengaluru	080-26 75 69 30	
Chennai	044-24 34 47 26,	24 35 95 07
Cochin	0484-237 70 04,	405 13 03
Guwahati	0361-254 36 69,	251 38 81
Hyderabad	040-27 55 53 83,	27 55 53 93
Jalandhar	0181-222 12 72	
Kolkata	033-22 27 43 84	
Lucknow	0522-220 99 16	
Mumbai	022-24 91 54 15,	24 92 78 69
Ranchi	0651-220 44 64	

PUBLISHED IN INDIA BY

FIREWALL MEDIA
(An Imprint of Laxmi Publications Pvt. Ltd.)

An ISO 9001:2008 Company
113, GOLDEN HOUSE, DARYAGANJ,
NEW DELHI - 110002, INDIA
Telephone : 91-11-4353 2500, 4353 2501
Fax : 91-11-2325 2572, 4353 2528
www.laxmipublications.com info@laxmipublications.com

C—
Printed at Repro Knowledgecast Limited, Thane

Foreword

It gives us great pleasure to introduce this collection of papers to be presented at the 2013 International Conference on Computer Graphics & Virtual Reality (CGVR'13), July 22 through 25, 2013, at The New Tropicana Hotel, Las Vegas, USA.

An important mission of the World Congress in Computer Science, Computer Engineering, and Applied Computing (a federated congress to which this conference is affiliated with) includes *"Providing a unique platform for a diverse community of constituents composed of scholars, researchers, developers, educators, and practitioners. The Congress makes concerted effort to reach out to participants affiliated with diverse entities (such as: universities, institutions, corporations, government agencies, and research centers/labs) from all over the world. The congress also attempts to connect participants from institutions that have* ***teaching*** *as their main mission with those who are affiliated with institutions that have* ***research*** *as their main mission. The congress uses a quota system to achieve its institution and geography diversity objectives."* By any definition of diversity, this congress is among the most diverse scientific meeting in USA. We are proud to report that this federated congress has authors and participants from 82 different nations representing variety of personal and scientific experiences that arise from differences in culture and values. As can be seen (see below), the program committee of this conference as well as the program committee of all other tracks of the federated congress are as diverse as its authors and participants.

The program committee would like to thank all those who submitted papers for consideration. About 60% of the submissions were from outside the United States. Each submitted paper was peer-reviewed by two experts in the field for originality, significance, clarity, impact, and soundness. In cases of contradictory recommendations, a member of the conference program committee was charged to make the final decision; often, this involved seeking help from additional referees. In addition, papers whose authors included a member of the conference program committee were evaluated using the double-blinded review process. One exception to the above evaluation process was for papers that were submitted directly to chairs/organizers of pre-approved sessions/workshops; in these cases, the chairs/organizers were responsible for the evaluation of such submissions. The overall paper acceptance rate for regular papers was 27%; 6% of the remaining papers were accepted as poster papers (at the time of this writing, we had not yet received the acceptance rate for a few individual tracks.)

We are very grateful to the many colleagues who offered their services in organizing the conference. In particular, we would like to thank the members of the Program Committee of CGVR'13, members of the congress Steering Committee, and members of the committees of federated congress tracks that have topics within the scope of CGVR. Many individuals listed below, will be requested after the conference to provide their expertise and services for selecting papers for publication (extended versions) in journal special issues as well as for publication in a set of research books (to be prepared for publishers including: Springer, Elsevier, BMC, and others).

- *Dr. Alireza Abbasi; School of Engineering and Information Technology, University of New South Wales (UNSW), Canberra, Australia*
- *Dr. Selim Aissi (World Congress Steering Committee); formerly, Chief Strategist - Security, Intel Corp., USA; Senior Business Leader & Head of Global Enterprise Security Architecture, Visa Corporation, USA*
- *Prof. Babak Akhgar (World Congress Steering Committee); Fellow of the British Computer Society, CITP; Professor of Informatics; Co-Director of CENTRIC (Centre of Excellence in Terrorism, Resilience, Intelligence & organised Crime research), Sheffield Hallam University, Sheffield, UK*
- *Prof. Nizar Al-Holou (World Congress Steering Committee); Professor and Chair, ECE Department; Vice Chair, IEEE/SEM-Computer Chapter; University of Detroit Mercy, Detroit, Michigan, USA*
- *Prof. Hamid R. Arabnia (World Congress Steering Committee); Professor, Computer Science; Editor-in-Chief, The Journal of Supercomputing (Springer); Elected Fellow, Int'l Society of Intelligent Biological Medicine (ISIBM); The University of Georgia, Department of Computer Science, USA*
- *Peyman Arebi; Assistant Professor, Department of Computer Engineering, Technical and Vocational University, Bushehr, Iran*
- *Prof. Juan Jose Martinez Castillo; Director of The Acantelys Research Group and Coordinator of the Computer Engineering Department, Universidad Gran Mariscal de Ayacucho, Venezuela*

- *Prof. Juan Cuadrado-Gallego; Universidad de Alcala, Edificio Politecnico, Madrid, Spain; Ecole de technologie superieure, University of Quebec, Canada*
- *Prof. Kevin Daimi (World Congress Steering Committee); Director, Computer Science and Software Engineering Programs; Department of Mathematics, Computer Science and Software Engineering; University of Detroit Mercy, Detroit, Michigan, USA*
- *Prof. Leonidas Deligiannidis; Professor, Computer Science, Wentworth Institute of Technology, MA, USA*
- *Prof. George Jandieri (World Congress Steering Committee); Georgian Technical University, Tbilisi, Georgia; Chief Scientist, The Institute of Cybernetics, Georgian Academy of Science, Georgia; Editorial Board Member: International Journal of Microwaves and Optical Technology, Georgia*
- *Prof. Dong Hwa Kim; Department of Electronic and Control Engineering, Hanbat National University, Korea; Visiting Professor, Budapest University of Technology and Economic, Hungary; International Einstein awardee for Scientific achievement (2010)*
- *Prof. Dattatraya V. Kodavade (World Congress Steering Committee); Head of Computer Science and Engineering, D.K.T.E Society's Textile & Engineering Institute, Ichalkaranji, Maharashtra State, India*
- *Prof. Kun Chang Lee (World Congress Steering Committee); Professor of MIS and WCU Professor of Creativity Science, Business School and Department of Interaction Science, Sungkyunkwan University, Korea*
- *Prof. George Markowsky (World Congress Steering Committee); Professor and Associate Director, School of Computing and Information Science; Chair Int'l Advisory Board of IEEE IDAACS; Director 2013 Northeast Collegiate Cyber Defense Competition; Cooperating Professor Mathematics and Statistics Department UMaine and School of Policy & International Affairs UMaine; University of Maine, Orono, Maine, USA*
- *Dr. Sara Moein; Editorial Board, International Journal of Science and Technology; Faculty of Engineering, MultiMedia University, Malaysia*
- *Dr. Ali Mostafaeipour; Industrial Engineering Department, Yazd University, Iran*
- *Dr. Saurabh Mukherjee; Banasthali University, Banasthali, Rajasthan, India*
- *Prof. G. N. Pandey (World Congress Steering Committee); Vice-Chancellor, Arunachal University of Studies, Arunachal Pradesh, India; Adjunct Professor, Indian Institute of Information Technology, Allahabad, India*
- *Prof. James J. (Jong Hyuk) Park (World Congress Steering Committee); Professor of Computer Science and Engineering, Seoul National University of Science and Technology (SeoulTech), Korea; President, KITCS; President, FTRA; Editor-in-Chiefs: HCIS, JoC and IJITCC Journals*
- *Dr. Liang Shi; Senior Researcher, McAfee, USA*
- *Ashu M. G. Solo, (Publicity Chair); Fellow of British Computer Society, Principal/R&D Engineer, Maverick Technologies America Inc., USA*
- *Prof. Fernando G. Tinetti (World Congress Steering Committee); School of Computer Science, Universidad Nacional de La Plata, La Plata, Argentina; Co-editor, Journal of CS and Technology (JCS&T)*
- *Dr. Predrag Tosic (World Congress Steering Committee); Microsoft, Washington, USA*
- *Prof. Vladimir Volkov (World Congress Steering Committee); The Bonch-Bruevich State University of Telecommunications, Saint-Petersburg, Russia*
- *Prof. Patrick Wang; Fellow of IAPR, ISIBM, WASE; Zijiang Chair Professor, ECNU, Shanghai and NTUST, Taipei, Taiwan; Founding President and CEO, Wang Teknowlogy Lab.; MIT Research Consultant; Harvard University, Adj. Faculty, USA; Northeastern University, Boston, MA, USA*
- *Prof. Jane You; The Hong Kong Polytechnic University, Hong Kong*

As Sponsors-at-large, partners, and/or organizers each of the followings (separated by semicolons) provided help for at least one track of the World Congress: Aldebaran Robotics Inc., USA (http://www.aldebaran-robotics.com); Altera Corporation, USA (http://www.altera.com/); Computer Science Research, Education, and Applications Press (CSREA); Impulse Accelerated Technologies, Inc., USA (http://www.impulseaccelerated.com/); NVIDIA Corporation, USA (http://www.nvidia.com/object/about-nvidia.html); Parallella Community, Supercomputing for Everyone, USA (http://forums.parallella.org/); Pico Computing, Inc., USA (http://picocomputing.com/); SemiWiki.com, The Semiconductor Wiki Project, USA (http://www.semiwiki.com/); Solarflare Communications, Inc., USA (http://www.solarflare.com/); Stream Computing, Performance Engineers, The Netherlands (http://streamcomputing.eu/); Taylor & Francis, UK (http://www.taylorandfrancis.com/); US Chapter of World Academy of Science (http://www.world-academy-of-science.org/) ; and WEBestSOL & Webest Solutions Ltd, UK (http://webestsol.com/). In addition, a number of university faculty members and their staff (names appear on the cover of the set of proceedings), several publishers of computer science and computer engineering books and journals, chapters and/or task forces of computer science associations/organizations from 5 countries, and developers of high-performance machines and systems provided significant help in organizing the conference as well as providing some resources. We are grateful to them all.

We express our gratitude to keynote, invited, and individual conference/tracks and tutorial speakers - the list of speakers appears on the conference web site. We would also like to thank the followings: UCMSS (Universal Conference Management Systems & Support, California, USA) for managing all aspects of the conference; Dr. Tim Field of APC for managing the printing of the proceedings; and the staff of the New Tropicana Hotel in Las Vegas for the professional service they provided. Last but not least, we would like to thank the Co-Editors of CGVR'13: Prof. Hamid R. Arabnia, Prof. Leonidas Deligiannidis, and Ashu M. G. Solo.

We present the proceedings of CGVR'13.

Steering Committee, 2013
http://www.world-academy-of-science.org/

Contents

SESSION: ANIMATION AND RELATED METHODOLOGIES

SESSION: VIRTUAL REALITY + COMPUTER GRAPHICS + RELATED METHODS

SESSION

ANIMATION AND RELATED METHODOLOGIES

Chair(s)

TBA

BodySpeech: A configurable facial and gesture animation system for speaking avatars

A. Fernández-Baena, M. Antonijoan, R. Montaño, A. Fusté, and J. Amores
Grup de Tecnologies Mèdia (GTM), La Salle - Universitat Ramon Llull, Barcelona, Catalonia, Spain

Abstract—*Speaking avatars are present in many Human Computer Interaction (HCI) applications. Their importance lies in communicative goals which entail interaction within other avatars in virtual worlds or in marketing where they have become useful in customer push strategies. Generating automatic and plausible animations from speech cues have become a challenge. We present BodySpeech, an automatic system to generate gesture and facial animations driven by speech. Body gestures are aligned with pitch accents and selected based on the strength relation between speech and body gestures. Concurrently, facial animation is generated for lip sync, adding emphatic hints according to intonation strength. Furthermore, we have implemented a tool for animators. This tool enables us to modify the detection of pitch accents and the intonation strength influence on output animations, allowing animators to define the activation of gestural performances.*

Keywords: human computer interaction; speaking avatars; gesture animation; facial animation

1. Introduction

Face-to-face communication has the goal of transmitting a message from one person to another. Besides the semantics, the way a message is transmitted can change how the receiver perceives it. Body language and facial animations accompany the acoustic signal of speech, and moreover, they enrich communication and make it believable [1]. So, in order to make human computer interfaces believable, we must take into account the characteristics of the visual speech. Given the difficulty of creating realistic speech animations automatically, many companies use hand-crafted animations. Generating specific animations for any speech utterance results in increased production time and budget. On the other hand, automatic synthesis of gestures according to speech have been broadly studied in the character animation research community [2][3], providing a solution for the mentioned issues.

In this paper we present BodySpeech: an automatic method to generate appropriate body gestures and facial expressions according to an arbitrary speech. The system is able to select body gestures based on speech intonation and to concatenate them generating a smooth motion stream. We use mocap data to create a motion graph [4] which is named gesture motion graph (GMG). The animation system generates a continuous stream of gestures by concatenating units included in the GMG. The gesture selection process is driven by prosodic features of pitch accents (changes in speech intonation) in speech. Pitch accents and their corresponding features (time and strength) are automatically detected based on [5]. For every pitch accent, the system selects a gesture phrase with an equivalent strength (see Figure 1). Moreover, gestures and pitch accents are aligned in time. At same time, facial animation is generated by lip sync. We use the blendshapes approach to create visemes (facial shapes) that are assigned to phonemes. Additionally, we modify output visemes based on pitch accent strength for each pitch accent.

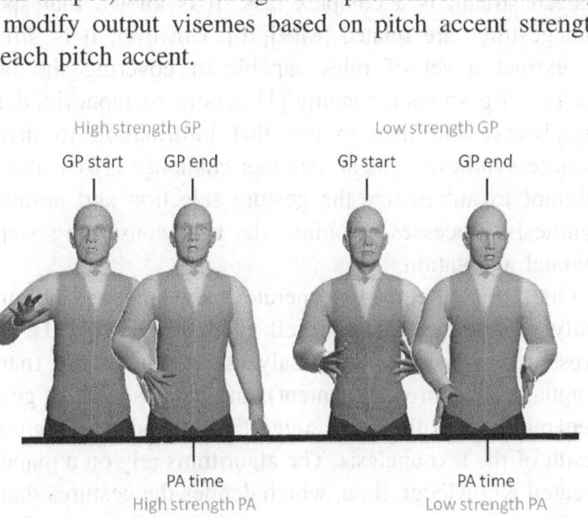

Fig. 1: BodySpeech. Gestural phrases (GP) are matched with pitch accents (PA) times and strength.

Moreover, we have implemented an application for animators that makes the generation of gesture and facial animations for speaking avatars easier. Using this application, animators can modify the speaker style by changing emphasis parameters. Emphasis of output animations depends on the frequency of performed gestures and the kinematic features of gestural movements. So, we facilitate the parameterized detection of pitch accents and determine how their strength affects output body and facial animations.

We summarize the related work in Section 2. Then, we describe the BodySpeech system in Section 3. Finally, we present an application for animators (Section 4) and conclude our work in Section 5.

This work expands on our prior work [6], primarily in

the automatization of gesture synthesis. In this paper we consider the automatic detection of pitch accents avoiding a manual annotation phase. This new way of detecting pitch accents is accompanied by a new pitch accent strength computation (more details in Section 3.3.1). Thanks to this, we have defined a new gesture-speech strength relation used in gesture selection (3.3.2.2). In terms of animation, we have enriched the GMG by reusing the input data to create more gestures (3.2.1). In addition, in order to avoid stroke modification (the most meaningful part of gestures) we have improved gesture temporal alignment with speech (3.3.2.1). Moreover, to improve output motion quality we use optimal blend length [7] to create blended transitions between gestures. Furthermore, as we have mentioned, we have added facial animation and implemented an authoring animation tool.

2. Related work

The generation of appropriate body language to a specific speech stream is a complex task. It is known that speech and gestures are related [8][9][10]. However, it is difficult to extract a set of rules capable of covering the broad variety of gestures taxonomy [1] (iconic, metaphoric, deictic and beats) and then to use that information to drive a gesture synthesis system. Another challenge arises from the attempt to automatize the gesture selection and animation synthesis processes, avoiding the time-consuming step of manual annotation.

One early attempt to generate body language automatically was presented by Casell et al. in BEAT [11]. They presented a system that analyzes an input text (natural language structure and content), and defines a set of gesture generation algorithms that suggest gestures depending on the result of the text analysis. The algorithms rely on a manually created Knowledge Base, which defines the gestures that are appropriate to certain actions or objects. Stone et al. [12] presented another automatic gesture synthesizer. However, in this case it uses a unit selection approach, and units are pieces of motion captured from real performances. This permits the generation of animation that naturally contains the subtleties of real human motion, which are hard to reproduce otherwise. Stone's synthesizer is limited to generating utterances present in a pre-defined grammar. Although this grammar can be extended as much as desired, the creation of this grammar requires some manual annotation. Neff et al. [13] proposed a novel system, that from an input text is capable of generating animations that recreate the style of a certain speaker. The process begins with a gesture selection step, which is driven by a statistical model created from performances of the speaker. In the next step the animation engine uses parameters that define the shape of gestures produced by the speaker and a set of predefined rules to produce the animation. The system is fully automatic but requires some annotation in the input text.

Other systems, do not rely in input text to generate animation but in prosodic parameters of speech directly. This allows to go a step further in adaptability because these parameters can be extracted either from the output of a text-to-speech synthesizer, as well from the audio of real speech. A limitation of these systems is that it is not possible to extract language structure or semantic content from prosody, and therefore they cannot be correlated with content of gestures. Moreover, prosodic-based gesture synthesizers usually only generate beat type gestures. Beats are a type of gesture that do not carry meaning, and their function is to emphasize words in a utterance [1]. It is known that prosody correlates well with emphasis [14], which suggests that beats are good candidates to be synthesized based on prosody. Levine et al. proposed two algorithms [15] [2] that automatically generate beat gestures based on input audio. Their systems use statistical models that shape the correlations between prosody and kinematic parameters of gestures. These models are used to select gestural units stored in a mocap database. Gestural units are composed of a single gestural phase. In a further work, Chiu et al. [3] presented a similar system but in this case units are composed by single animation frames. This permits the generation of a greater variety of gestures at cost of animation realism. Our approach is similar to Chiu's and Levine's in the fact that it uses prosody to select motion units from a database. However, the unit selection process is not governed by a statistical model but by a set of rules. This allows greater parametrization of the process, which in turn provides greater control of the output.

3. BodySpeech

3.1 Overview

The animation system is divided into two stages: an off-line preprocessing step and a runtime unsupervised step. Figure 2 shows an outline of the whole system. In the first stage, gesture mocap data is arranged in a motion graph structure as described in Section 3.2.1. On the other hand, we associate visemes (mouth shapes) with phonemes. Vowel phonemes have more than one associated viseme in order to capture emphasis in facial animation. Visemes parameterization is further explained in Section 3.2.2.

The second stage is where the output animation is generated. Speech is used to drive both gesture synthesis and facial animation. Input speech is analyzed in order to detect pitch accents (time occurrence and strength indicator) and the phoneme transcription of the message (Section 3.3.1). Pitch accents drive gesture synthesis by selecting the most appropriate gesture unit for each one depending on strength levels (see more details in Section 3.3.2). We use gestural phrases as gesture units. A gestural phrase [16] consists of the following phases: stroke (obligatory phase where it is contained the 'expression of the gesture'), preparation (movement that leads to the beginning of the stroke) and

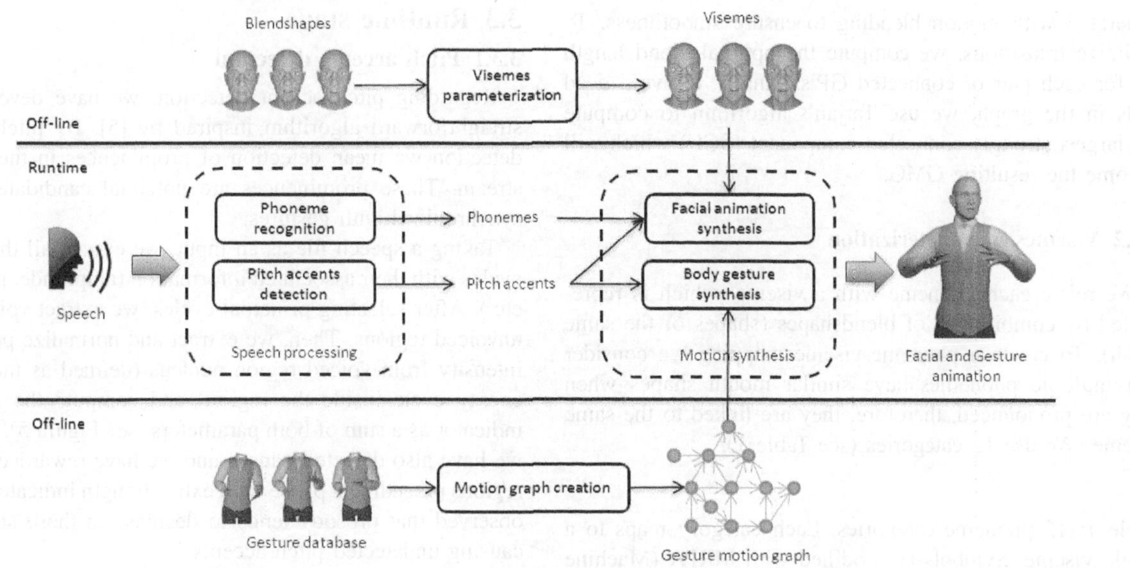

Fig. 2: System overview. The off-line stage is used to generate a motion graph (at the bottom) and a set of visemes (on top). Then, body and facial animation are obtained from a speech signal in the runtime stage (on the middle).

retraction (body parts are moved to the rest position). Moreover, gestural phrases may include hold phases which are temporary cessations of movement. At the same time, phonemes intervals are matched with visemes to generate facial animation. Additionally, visemes are modified based on pitch accent strength indicators (see Section 3.3.3).

3.2 Off-line stage

3.2.1 Motion graph creation

A labeled gesture motion database is used to construct a motion graph [4]. This database consists of 6 clips that last slightly more than one minute each, in which an amateur actor with mocap recording experience was asked to perform an improvised monologue with a concrete speaking style and performing only beat gestures. We choose neutral and aggressive style in order to obtain a broad variety of gestures with different strengths. Gestural phrases and their corresponding gesture phases are annotated in this database. Also, stroke apexes (the maximum extension point) are annotated. So, we use gestural phrases (GP) motion clips to populate a gesture motion graph (GMG). Also, stroke phases are extracted and added as new gestural phrases. In this way, we maximize the number of gestural phrases allowing more variety in gesture synthesis.

A GMG is defined by N for the set of nodes (GP's), E for the set of edges (transitions) and $W(E)$ for the set of edge weights (transition parameters). First, we connect all the consecutive GP's from the original database with a directional edge. Then, we create new edges between non-consecutive GP's. Transitioning between non consecutive

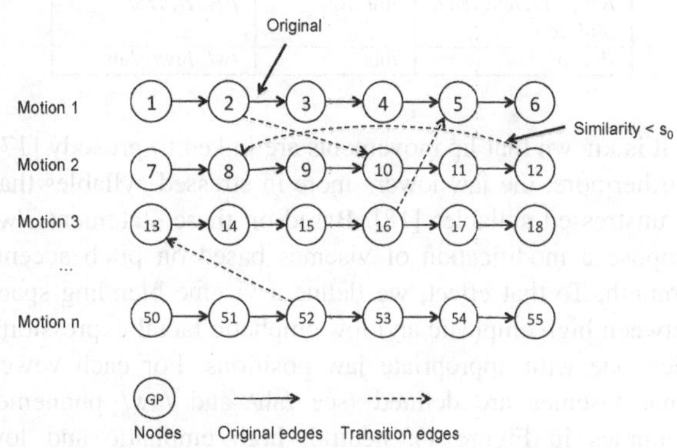

Fig. 3: Edge generation in gesture motion graph. We create an edge connecting two gestural phrases if they are consecutive in the original recordings (original edges) or their posture similarity is below s_0 (transition edges).

gesture phrases can produce jerky motions if GPs extreme postures are not similar enough. Therefore, we compute posture similarity between initial and ending frames from all motion clips in the graph using joint angles distance metric [4]. As a consequence, we create edges when the similarity value is lower than a threshold s_0 (see Figure 3). In order to search the appropriate gestures in the motion graph and to generate smooth transitions between GP's, we weight the edges of the graph with posture similarity values. We scale posture similarity values to [0,1], where 1 is the specified threshold s_0. Transitions between GP's are generated with motion blending to ensure smoothness. To optimize transitions, we compute the optimal blend length [7] for each pair of connected GP's. Finally, to avoid dead ends in the graph, we use Tarjan's algorithm to compute the largest strongly connected component (SCC) which will become the resulting GMG.

3.2.2 Visemes parameterization

We relate each phoneme with a viseme, which is represented by combination of blendshapes (shapes of the same mesh). To create a phoneme-viseme mapping we consider that multiple phonemes have similar mouth shapes when they are pronounced, therefore, they are linked to the same viseme. We use 15 categories (see Table 1).

Table 1: 15 phoneme categories. Each category maps to a single viseme. Symbols are codified with MRPA (Machine Readable Phonemic Alphabet).

/pau/	/r/	/k/, /g/, /ng/
/ae/, /ax/, /ah/, /aa/	/f/, /v/	/ch/, /sh/, /jh/
/ao/, /y/, /iy/, /ih/, /ay/, /aw/	/ow/, /oy/	/n/, /d/, /t/, /l/
/ey/, /eh/, /el/, /em/, /en/, /er/	/th/, /dh/	/s/, /z/, /zh/
/b/, /p/, /m/	/hh/	/w/, /uw/, /uh/

It is known that lip movements are linked to prosody [17]. Furthermore, the jaw lowers more in stressed syllables than in unstressed syllables [18]. Based on these statements, we propose a modification of visemes based on pitch accents strength. To that effect, we define a viseme blending space between high emphatic and low emphatic facial expressions, each one with appropriate jaw positions. For each vowel, three visemes are defined (see /ah/ and /aw/ phonemes examples in Figure 4): neutral, high emphatic and low emphatic.

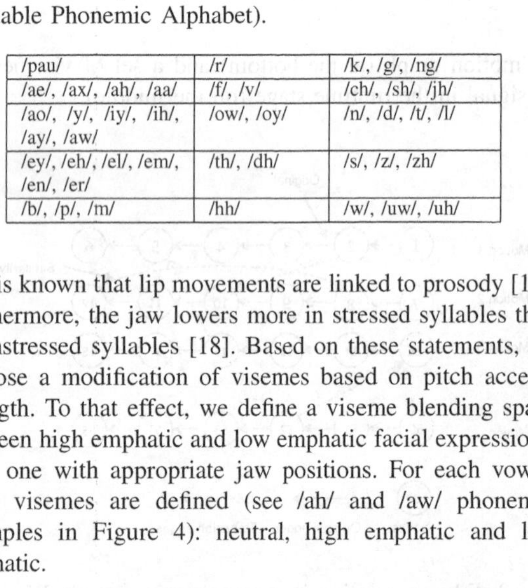

Fig. 4: Emphatic visemes for /ah/ and /aw/ phonemes.

3.3 Runtime stage

3.3.1 Pitch accents detection

Regarding pitch accent detection, we have developed a straightforward algorithm inspired by [5]. By pitch accent detection we mean detection of prominences in the speech stream. These prominences are potential candidates to be synchronized with gestures.

Taking a speech file as an input, we extract all the signal cycles with their associated information (amplitude, position, etc.). After selecting principal cycles, we extract voiced and unvoiced regions. Then, we extract and normalize pitch and intensity from voiced region nucleus (defined as maximum energy cycle inside the region) and compute the strength indicator as a sum of both parameters (see Figure 5). Finally, we have also detected pauses and we have rewarded voiced regions preceding a pause with extra strength indicator, as we observed that prosody tends to decrease in these situations causing undetected pitch accents.

Final pitch accents are detected according to the extracted strength indicators of the voiced region nucleus. Specifically, they are chosen depending on two tunable constraint parameters: strength indicator threshold and time difference threshold. Basically, the strength indicator threshold represents what percentage of the nucleus are pitch accents candidates (taking as a reference maximum strength indicator), and the time difference threshold defines how close pitch accents can be. If two pitch accent candidates are too close according to this parameter, we keep the one with the greater strength indicator. Finally, the pitch accents strength indicator is expressed in a [0,1] scale, taking as 1 the maximum strength indicator of the series.

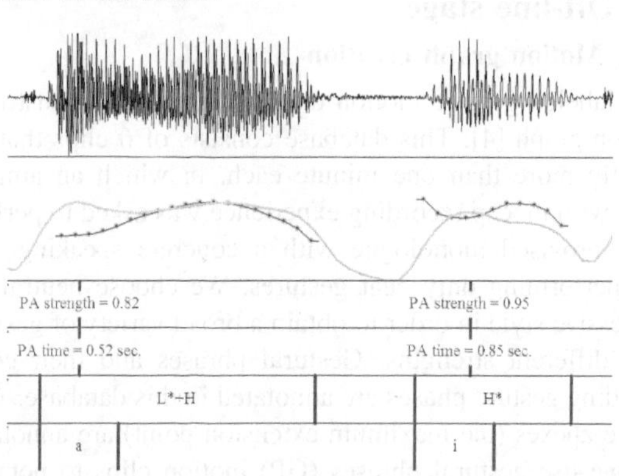

Fig. 5: Pitch accents detection. On top, there is the speech signal. Below, intensity (green) and pitch (blue) curves are displayed. In addition, pitch accent (PA) strength and time are shown. At the bottom, the intonation is represented (using the ToBI system [19]) with the affected vowel. The image was created thanks to the Praat software [20].

Furthermore, speech is analyzed to extract the phoneme transcription. So, we obtain a sequence of phonemes with its type definition and timestamps. For each phoneme, initial time and final time are detected.

3.3.2 Body gesture synthesis

As we have explained, gesture synthesis is driven by pitch accents. Distances between consecutive pitch accent times define the duration of selected GPs, and pitch accents strength are related to GP's strength. We adopt FMDistance [21] to define GP strength using the reported parameters in [6]. Moreover, it is only computed for the stroke phase and it is normalized to [0,1]. Then, we iteratively evaluate each pitch accent and seek the most appropriate GP for each one. Gesture performance starts with a rest pose (which is also included in the motion graph as a node) and we use a breadth-first search algorithm to traverse the graph according to a proposed cost metric. Selected GP's are concatenated by motion blending to obtain a smooth motion stream. To finish the animation, the avatar returns to the rest pose.

a) Temporal alignment: Before computing the cost metric, candidate GPs (connected to the current node) are warped to temporally align them with the current pitch accent time. Our objective is to make the apex of the stroke coincide with the pitch accent time. However, it is known that gesture apexes are not exactly aligned with pitch accents [9]. In order to allow this de-synchronization, we compute an anticipation time for each pitch accent as a random value within a pre-defined window (from -0.03 to 0.22 seconds [6]) .

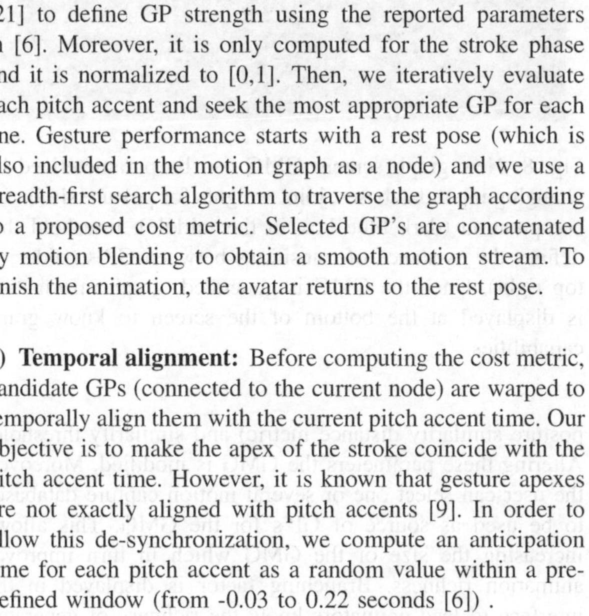

Fig. 6: Gesture alignment. Body gestures are aligned with pitch accents by modifying their length. The goal is to match stroke apexes with pitch accents times (t), taking into account anticipation times (T_a). We consider two cases: only stroke (on the left) and gestural phrase (on the right).

Furthermore, it is important to not modify strokes because they are the most significative part of gestures and emphasis relation in gesture selection is based on them. Hence, we manage two cases to align GPs with pitch accents times: 'only stroke' and 'gestural phrase'. 'Only stroke' means that the gestural phrase is formed by a unique stroke, in this case, stroke length will be modified. 'Gestural phrase' case means that GP has more phases besides the stroke, so, we modify phases which are not the stroke phase. Then, GP length (and its phases length) is computed by taking into account the mentioned cases, anticipation time and blending length (included as an edge weight in GMG) between the current node and the candidate one. Therefore, we obtain a w warping factor (original length divided by target length) for each candidate GP. In the 'only stroke' case, we consider the stroke length to compute w. On the other hand, we consider the sum of non-stroke phases lengths in the 'gestural phrase' case.

b) Gestural phrase selection: Our cost metric is based on: length similarity between a GP and the interval to fill (time cost), posture similarity between candidate GP and the previous one (smooth cost) and pitch accent strength-stroke strength relation (emphasis cost). As a result, we define our cost metric as

$$C(e(n_i, n_j), pa_k) = C_{smooth} + C_{emphasis} + C_{time} \quad (1)$$

where n_i is the previous GP, n_j is a candidate GP, and pa_k is the k-th pitch accent in speech stream. Smooth cost (C_{smooth}) is directly the posture similarity edge weight. Emphasis cost ($C_{emphasis}$) is the absolute difference between pitch accent strength indicator and gesture strength indicator. We recompute gesture strength indicator in the 'only stroke' time alignment case due to its duration, and consequently, its strength has changed. Time cost (C_{time}) is defined by

$$C_{time} = \begin{cases} w' & \text{if} \quad min < w < max \\ p & \text{otherwise} \end{cases} \quad (2)$$

where w' is the normalized warping factor from $[min, max]$ to [0,1]. We use min and max to not deteriorate motion quality by excessive changes on the original lengths. p is a penalty parameter that we use for penalizing GP's that exceed boundaries, avoiding their selection. Depending on the case of warping min and max take different values: 0.8 and 1.2 respectively for the 'gestural phrase' case, and 0.9 and 1.1 for the 'only stroke' case. Penalty parameter p is set to 10.

Once we have selected a gesture (the one with the minimum cost), this is concatenated with the previous one by linear motion blending. We use start-end blending scheme [7] and the blending length included in the edge weights of the graph.

3.3.3 Facial animation synthesis

We use phoneme transcription of the speech message to match phonemes with defined visemes. As usual, coarticulation between phonemes is generated by interpolating mesh points of visemes during initial and final times of phonemes. To include emphasis in facial expressions, we modify vowel visemes by blending them with its emphatic visemes. This only occurs when a vowel phoneme matchs with a pitch accent. We relate pitch accent strength indicator with the amount of weight from neutral and high/low emphatic visemes. Pitch accent strength indicator is expressed in a 0 to 1 scale, so, we associate 0 values to low emphatic viseme, and 1 to high emphatic viseme as illustrated in Figure 7. So, pitch accent strength indicators that are lower than 0.5 will be represented by a combination of neutral and low emphatic viseme. Otherwise, neutral and high emphatic visemes will be used in the morphing process. In this way, we obtain the appropriate viseme according to speech intonation.

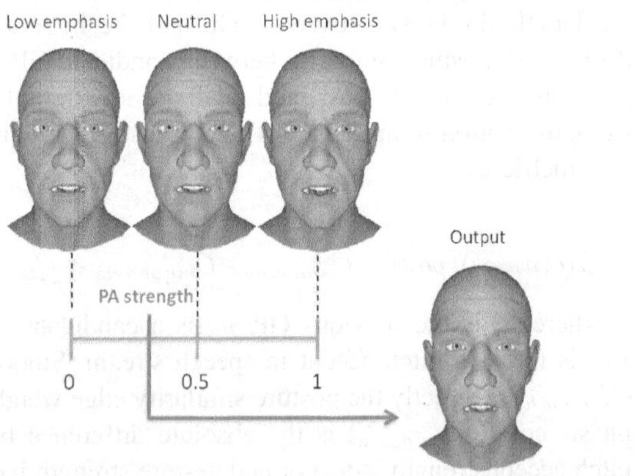

Fig. 7: Output viseme generation for pitch accents. Pitch accent (PA) strength is used to weight low emphatic, neutral and high emphatic visemes in the morphing process. In this example, higher emphatic visemes have more opened mouths.

4. Implementation

We have implemented the BodySpeech system as a plugin for the Unity3D game engine [22]. The Unity editor was used to create a visual interface that allows generating animations by selecting input speech audio files. In addition, the application uses Microsoft Speech API (SAPI) [23] to detect speech phonemes, and the Tagarela plugin [24] for facial morphing.

The application is able to parameterize the processes of gesture motion graph creation and viseme generation. Also, the process that synthesizes animations can be parameterized in order to modify emphasis, both for gesture and facial animations. This way,, animators can adjust output animations to satisfy plot requirements. The application is divided into three parts: New profile, Load profile and Player. New profile permits to generate a custom GMG (see Figure 8) and visemes; Load profile allows to select a saved profile; and Player lets to replay previous generated animations.

The process of generating new GMG's can be configured with the following parameters: joint weights (they are used in

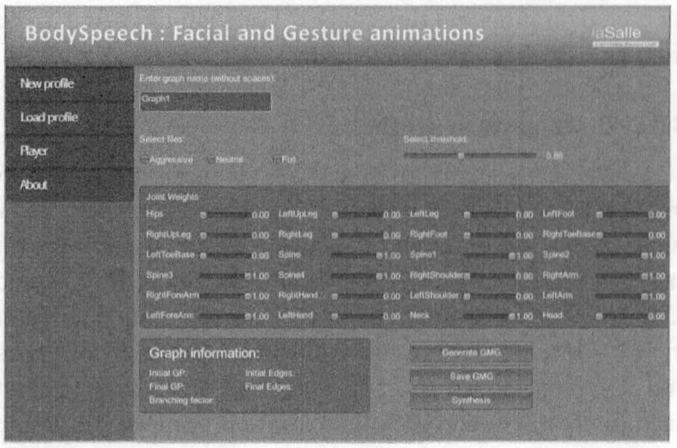

Fig. 8: New graph screen. GMG can be parameterized by changing input databases, joint weights for posture similarity computation (dark blue box in the middle), threshold that defines the existance of transitions between GP's (slider on top right). Once the GMG is generated, graph information is displayed at the bottom of the screen to know graph capabilities.

posture similarity distance metric) and similarity threshold. Altering these parameters the GMG is modified. Moreover, the user can select one or several motion capture databases to be used as source of GP's for the GMG. This allows increasing the size of the GMG which in turn improves animation richness. Branching factor is displayed in the interface to lead animators know the richness of generated graphs. Also, visemes can be customized by changing the weights of former blendshapes.

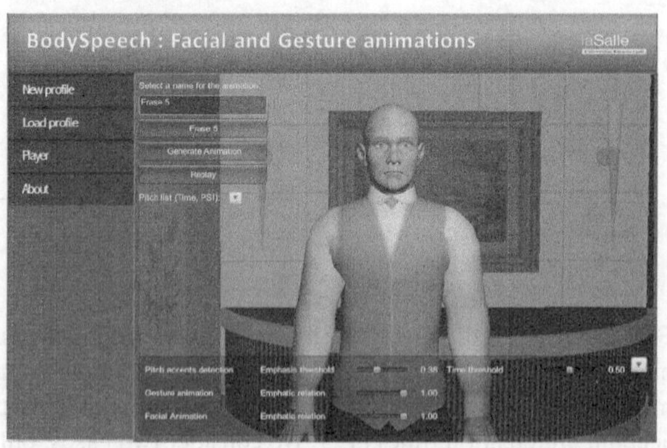

Fig. 9: Synthesis screen. On the upper-left corner, there are the buttons to select an audio and generate the animations. At the bottom, there are the configurable pitch accent detection parameters, and sliders for adjusting gestural or facial animation emphasis.

As explained in Section 3.3.1, pitch accent detection can be parameterized by changing the strength indicator threshold and the time difference threshold. These two parameters can be modified in the application affecting the frequency of detected pitch accents and gestures. A greater gesture frequency is perceived as a more emphatic animation. Moreover, emphasis of gesture and facial animations can be also be adjusted independently with two moving sliders. The gesture slider modifies the amount of strength that is added or subtracted to pitch accent strength (from -1 to +1). 0 denotes that the input pitch accent strength remains equal, positive values increase pitch accent strength value up to 1, while negative values decrease strength value down to -1. This permits the generation of more prominent gestures from a low emphatic speech, or contrarily, to relax gesticulation in a high emphatic speech. Similarly, facial animation emphasis is controlled by an analogous slider.

5. Conclusions and future work

In this paper, we have presented an automatic method to generate body gestures and facial animation according to speech input. Our animation system is based on motion graphs and lip sync techniques. Gesture animation stream is produced by concatenating gesture phrases aligned with pitch accents. Gestures are selected in order to maintain motion smoothness, preserve as many original motion clips as possible and obey emphasis relation with speech. Lip sync is generated following a standard algorithm. However, we relate speech strength with facial expressions to improve realism. Moreover, we have implemented a tool for animators that allows controlling the output animations via parameterization. A set of straightforward parameters are presented which permit a change in animation emphasis by adjusting pitch accents detection or emphasis relation between gestures/visemes with speech.

As future work, we plan to improve facial animation synthesis by studying the relationship between speech intonation and facial expressions. In addition, we plan to include independent head motion [25] and finger motion [26] to further increase realism of the overall animations.

Acknowledgements

This work was supported by the CENIT program number CEN-20101019, granted by the Ministry of Science and Innovation of Spain.

References

[1] D. McNeill, *Hand and Mind: What Gestures Reveal about Thought.* Chicago: University of Chicago Press, 1992.

[2] S. Levine, P. Krähenbühl, S. Thrun, and V. Koltun, "Gesture controllers," *ACM Trans. Graph.*, vol. 29, no. 4, pp. 124:1–124:11, July 2010.

[3] C.-C. Chiu and S. Marsella, "How to train your avatar: a data driven approach to gesture generation," in *Proceedings of the 10th international conference on Intelligent virtual agents*, ser. IVA'11. Berlin, Heidelberg: Springer-Verlag, 2011, pp. 127–140.

[4] J. Lee, J. Chai, P. S. A. Reitsma, J. K. Hodgins, and N. S. Pollard, "Interactive control of avatars animated with human motion data," *ACM Trans. Graph.*, vol. 21, pp. 491–500, July 2002.

[5] O. Maeran, V. Piuri, and G. Storti Gajani, "Speech recognition through phoneme segmentation and neural classification," in *Instrumentation and Measurement Technology Conference, 1997. IMTC/97. Proceedings. Sensing, Processing, Networking., IEEE*, vol. 2, May, pp. 1215–1220 vol.2.

[6] A. Fernández-Baena, R. Montaño, M. Antonijoan, A. Roversi, D. Miralles, and F. Alías, "Gesture synthesis adapted to speech emphasis," *Speech Communication (Special Issue on Gesture and Speech in Interaction). In press.*

[7] J. Wang and B. Bodenheimer, "Synthesis and evaluation of linear motion transitions," *ACM Trans. Graph.*, vol. 27, pp. 1:1–1:15, March 2008. [Online]. Available: http://doi.acm.org/10.1145/1330511.1330512

[8] D. McNeill, "So you think gestures are nonverbal?" *Psychological Review*, vol. 92, no. 3, pp. 350–371, 1985.

[9] D. Loehr, "Gesture and intonation," Ph.D. dissertation, Georgetown University, 2004.

[10] T. Leonard and F. Cummins, "The temporal relation between beat gestures and speech," *Language and Cognitive Processes*, vol. 26, no. 10, pp. 1457–1471, 2011. [Online]. Available: http://www.tandfonline.com/doi/abs/10.1080/01690965.2010.500218

[11] J. Cassell, "Beat: The behavior expression animation toolkit." ACM Press, 2001, pp. 477–486.

[12] M. Stone, D. DeCarlo, I. Oh, C. Rodriguez, A. Stere, A. Lees, and C. Bregler, "Speaking with hands: creating animated conversational characters from recordings of human performance," *ACM Trans. Graph.*, vol. 23, no. 3, pp. 506–513, Aug. 2004. [Online]. Available: http://doi.acm.org/10.1145/1015706.1015753

[13] M. Neff, M. Kipp, I. Albrecht, and H.-P. Seidel, "Gesture modeling and animation based on a probabilistic re-creation of speaker style," *ACM Trans. Graph.*, vol. 27, no. 1, pp. 5:1–5:24, Mar. 2008. [Online]. Available: http://doi.acm.org/10.1145/1330511.1330516

[14] J. Terken, "Fundamental frequency and perceived prominence of accented syllables," *The Journal of the Acoustical Society of America*, vol. 89, no. 4, pp. 1768–1776, 1991.

[15] S. Levine, C. Theobalt, and V. Koltun, "Real-time prosody-driven synthesis of body language," *ACM Trans. Graph.*, vol. 28, no. 5, pp. 172:1–172:10, Dec. 2009. [Online]. Available: http://doi.acm.org/10.1145/1618452.1618518

[16] A. Kendon, "Gesture and speech: two aspects of the process utterances," *Nonverbal Communication and Language*, pp. 207–227, 1980.

[17] E. Cvejic, J. Kim, and C. Davis, "It's all the same to me: Prosodic discrimination across speakers and face areas," in *Speech Prosody 2010-Fifth International Conference*, 2010.

[18] K. de Jong, M. Beckman, and J. Edwards, "The interplay between prosodic structure and coarticulation." *Lang Speech*, vol. 36 (Pt 2-3).

[19] K. Silverman, M. Beckman, J. Pierrehumbert, M. Ostendorf, C. Wightman, and J. Hirschberg, "TOBI: A standard scheme for labeling prosody," in *Proceedings of ICSLP-92*, Banff, October 1992, pp. 867–879.

[20] P. Boersma and D. Weenink, "Praat: doing phonetics by computer [computer program]. (v.5.2.29)," retrieved 12 July 2011 from http://www.praat.org/, 2011.

[21] K. Onuma, C. Faloutsos, and J. K. Hodgins, "FMDistance: A fast and effective distance function for motion capture data," in *Short Papers Proceedings of EUROGRAPHICS*, 2008.

[22] Unity, "Unity3d," 2013. [Online]. Available: http://www.unity3d.com/

[23] Microsoft, "Microsoft speech api," 2013. [Online]. Available: http://www.microsoft.com/en-us/download/details.aspx?id=10121

[24] R. Pegorari, "Tagarela - open source lip sync system for unity," 2013. [Online]. Available: http://rodrigopegorari.net/blog/?p=241

[25] C. Busso, Z. Deng, U. Neumann, and S. Narayanan, "Natural head motion synthesis driven by acoustic prosodic features: Virtual humans and social agents," *Comput. Animat. Virtual Worlds*, vol. 16, no. 3-4, pp. 283–290, July 2005. [Online]. Available: http://dx.doi.org/10.1002/cav.v16:3/4

[26] S. Jörg, J. Hodgins, and A. Safonova, "Data-driven finger motion synthesis for gesturing characters," *ACM Trans. Graph.*, vol. 31, no. 6, pp. 189:1–189:7, Nov. 2012. [Online]. Available: http://doi.acm.org/10.1145/2366145.2366208

Animating TTS Messages in Android using Open-Source Tools

Ronald Yu
School of Computer Science and Engineering
University of California, Irvine
ronaly1@uci.edu

Tong Lai Yu
School of Computer Science and Engineering
California State University, San Bernardino
tyu@csusb.edu

Ihab Zbib
School of Computer Science and Engineering
California State University, San Bernardino
zbibi@csusb.edu

ABSTRACT

We describe in this paper how to use open-source resources to design and implement an Android application that renders a three-dimensional model of a human head to animate the lip movements of human speech from input text. The application utilizes the Android Text-To-Speech (TTS) engine[1] to convert any input text, which can be entered by the user in a text box or chosen from a menu of predefined messages, to human speech in English. Animation of the speech is carried out by a 3D graphics model of a human head composed of polygon meshes[20]. Blender[7, 30], a popular open-source graphics suite, is employed to create the 3D model and save its mesh data in the COLLAborative Design Activity (COLLADA) format[22], which is also an open graphics format.

We use Java language to develop a parser[25, 42] to extract coordinates of polygons from a COLLADA file and organize the data into a format that can be rendered effectively by OpenGL ES, the graphics rendering library used by Android. The producer-consumer paradigm is employed to synchronize the animated lip movements and the speech generated by TTS. When the application is lying idle, it moves the head randomly to simulate other facial expressions such as blinking the eyes and yawning.

Keywords

Open-source, 3D Graphics, Animation, Text-To-Speech, TTS, Android

1. INTRODUCTION

Open-source software has been playing a critical role in the advent of technology. A lot of breakthroughs in technology development and application such as Watson's Jeopardy win[5] and the phenomenal 3D movie Avatar[4] are based on open-source software. It is a significant task to explore the usage of available open-source tools to develop software applications for research or for commercial use[40, 41]. The Android application reported in this paper is developed with free software resources, which are mainly open-source.

Mobile devices have become ubiquitous and in the last couple of years, Android, an open-source software stack for running mobile devices, has become the dominant platform of many mobile devices such as mobile phones and smart phones[14]. There has been exponential growth in mobile applications in recent years. Speech simulation is one of the areas that enjoy rapid growth, and a significant amount of research has been done on speech animation using 3D graphics models[32]. The video compression standard MPEG-4 also has specifications on facial animation for synthesized speech[28, 13].

Though speech simulation is still an ongoing research topic, it already has numerous commercial applications including game development and customer service[6], and it contributes to both the developments of acoustic and visual applications[12, 9].

Our work reported in this paper develops and merges the audio and visual technologies into one application by making use of open-source technologies. The main tool we use for rendering graphics is OpenGL for embedded systems (ES). The graphics library OpenGL[33] is the industry standard for developing 2D and 3D graphics applications[2, 8], and OpenGL ES[23, 3, 27] is OpenGL modified for embedded systems. There is a major difference between OpenGL ES 1.X and OpenGL ES 2.X. While the 1.X version shares the same functionality and syntax of the traditional OpenGL APIs and, like early OpenGL, has a fixed pipeline and operates as a state machine, the 2.X version has adopted a programmable pipeline architecture that allows users to program vertex and fragment shaders[24, 31], the equivalent of OpenGL Shading Language (GLSL)[18]. The vertex shader is responsible for processing geometry. The fragment shader works at the pixel level, processing incoming fragments to produce colors including transparency.

Mobile devices are characterized by small display size[29], limited memory capacity and limited computing power. All of these aspects affect the graphic animation experience of the mobile user. These limitations make the design and implementation of a TTS animation application in a mobile device very different from that of an application running on

WORLDCOMP'13:CGVR13 July 22–25, 2013, Las Vegas, Nevada, USA.

a desktop PC.

Another problem one must address is the audio-video synchronization. For traditional video compression of natural scenes, MPEG standard uses timestamps to synchronize audio and video streams[19]. MPEG-4 also addresses coding of digital hybrids of natural and synthetic, aural and visual information[28, 32]. Doenges et al. mentioned in their paper[13] that special attention must be paid to the synchronization of acoustic speech information with coherent visible articulatory movements of the speakers mouth in MPEG-4 synthetic/natural hybrid coding (SNHC) for animated mixed media delivery. However, they did not present the details of synchronization in the paper. Our synchronization problem of video and audio is different from that of MPEG-4 as our application does not involve any data encoding and decoding, and data transmission. Therefore, we do not use timestamps to synchronize audio and video. Instead, the synchronization is done using the producer-consumer paradigm[35], which works effectively in this situation.

The application is developed for Android-based mobile devices. Android provides a Text-to-Speech (TTS) engine (PICO) with limited APIs[1]. The main thread of the application presents a text box to the user for entering texts; prepared sample texts are also available as items on the application menu, and a sample can be chosen by clicking on a button of the menu. The input text is used for the speech simulator that plays the sound using the Android TTS APIs and renders the corresponding visemes while performing a lip-synchronization action, keeping the audio and video synchronized. Visemes, which can be considered as visual counterpart of phonemes in audio, are visually distinct mouth, teeth, and tongue articulations for a language.

Besides the main thread, the application has three other threads. One of them is responsible for voice synthesis and speech simulation by making use of the Android Text-to-Speech(TTS) engine[1]. Another thread controls the 3D rendering and animation of a human head. This thread implements the OpenGL ES function calls and has to decide which object to render based on the input data. The last thread is the input text thread that handles the insertion of the data into the text buffer. This thread implements the producer in the Producer-Consumer problem. Figure 1 is a UML diagram showing these components and their connections, where the TTS Thread is Consumer 1 and the Animation Thread is Consumer 2.

2. GRAPHICS 3D MODEL

The 3D model is initially imported from Google SketchUp 3DWarehouse[16] and is shown in Figure 2. We use the free version of Sketchup[36], a 3D drawing tool, to convert it to a COLLADA file, which can be then imported by Blender[7, 30]. Blender is a free 3D graphic suite for creating, rendering and animating graphics models[30]. It supports a variety of formats such as COLLADA(.dae), Wavefront(.obj), 3D Studio(.3ds), and others.

To generate a new facial expression, the model is modified by deforming the mesh, and a different copy is created and passed to the COLLADA parser to create a metafile. The viseme, or the shape of the mouth that corresponds to each phoneme, is based on the lip-sync phonetic-based animation[38, 15] used in animation movies. Figure 3 shows the lip shapes for phonemes that we have adopted.

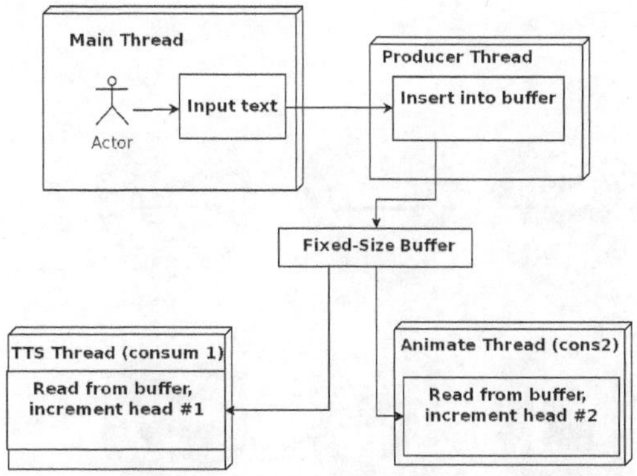

Figure 1: Components Diagram

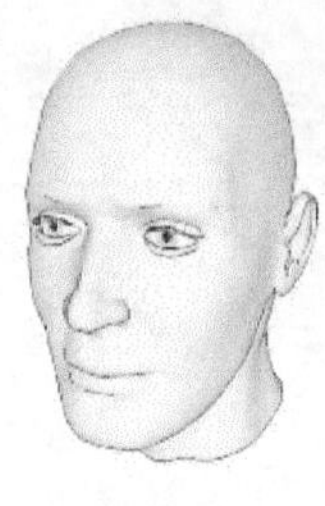

Figure 2: Model From Google 3DWarehouse

In addition to the mouth shapes, other facial expressions are created to help simulate a more human-like agent. These facial expressions include eye blinking, eyebrow movements and yawning. These expressions are presented to keep the user entertained when the application is idle. Figure 4 shows the Android emulator running the 3D Face at rest position.

Java is used to develop a COLLADA parser[25], which parses a COLLADA file and extracts the necessary information for rendering and animating the graphic models. The faces of the model are meshes of polygons of three or more edges. Because OpenGL ES 1.0 can only render triangles, the parser has to extract the indices of every polygon, convert them into triangles, and recalculate the normal vector for every triangle by performing a cross product of the vectors along two of the triangle's edges.

Since the COLLADA file is essentially an XML document, the parser needs to make use of an XML library to carry out the parsing. Java APIs provide wide support for XML parsing and a variety of libraries to choose from such as JAXP, JDOM and SAX. Most of these libraries support the XML Path Language (XPath) [17]. While the Document Object Model (DOM) [39] is a more complete tree structure representation of the document, XPath is a straightforward language that allows the selection of a subset of nodes based on their location in the document [17]. The parsing program described here makes use of the Java package *javax.xml.xpath* to extract the necessary nodes from the

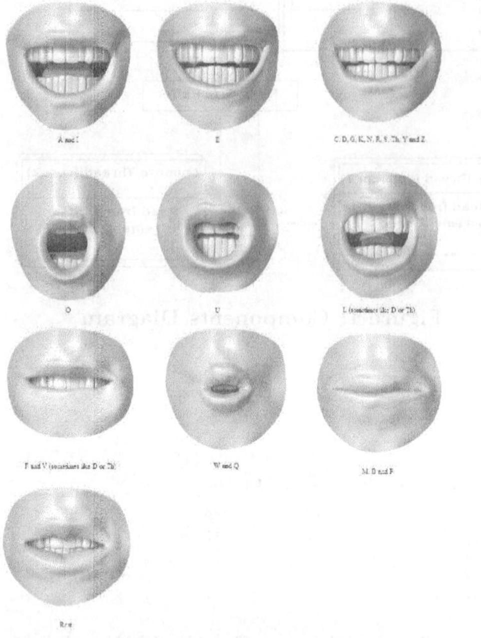

Figure 3: Preston Blair Phoneme Series

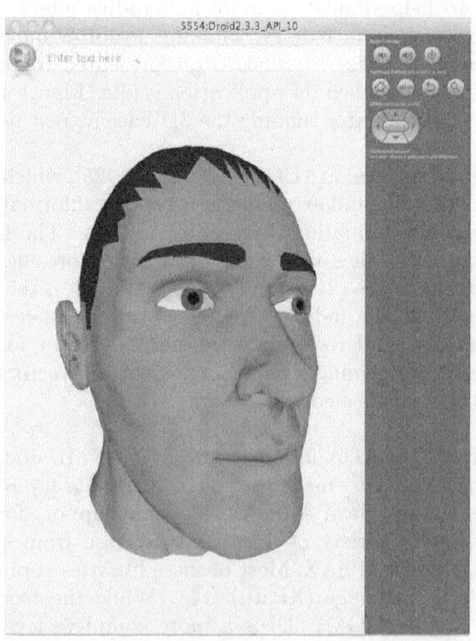

Figure 4: Resting Position

COLLADA document.

The parser parses the data of a COLLADA file into a meta-file containing a set of vertices coordinates, their normal vectors, the indices of the triangle and normalized color codes. The following data sample is an example of the data of a meta-file.

Meta-file Data Sample:

```
#upper_head.dae
object:base_039-mesh
{
  vertices:2517
  {
    0 2.8f,1.38f,-0.66f,
    1 2.83f,1.31f,-0.72f,
    2 2.78f,1.31f,-0.72f,
    ...
  }
  normals:2517
  {
    0 0.02f,0.62f,-0.78f,
    1 0.03f,1.0f,-0.08f,
    2 -0.74f,0.26f,-0.61f,
    ...
  }
  indices:4311
  {
    0 0,1,2,
    1 3,4,5,
    2 6,2,1,
    ...
  }
  materials:6
  {
    0 3509,0.51f,0.37f,0.31f,1.0f,
    1 50,0.41f,0.41f,0.41f,1.0f,
    2 690,0.13f,0.0f,0.0f,1.0f,
    ...
  }
}
```

The data labeled materials represent the color codes in red, green, and blue (RGB) of the affected faces. The first number is the table index and the second number indicates the number of faces that this color is applied to. The next three numbers are normalized RGB color codes. The color codes are normalized by dividing every component by 255. And the last number is the transparency, with values between 0 and 1, a value of 1 meaning opaque, and 0 meaning total transparency.

Every facial expression requires a separate graphic file that has to be loaded by the Android application. In order to reduce the amount of data, if the meta-file is a variation of the base model, the parser will compare it to the base model and export only the differences. This helps to reduce the start-up time of the Android application, as it does not need to create a different graphic object for every variation. The application can duplicate the original model and apply the changes in coordinates.

As mentioned earlier, OpenGL ES is the industry standard for embedded 3D graphics applications. This project makes use of OpenGL 1.0, which is supported by most of the commercial devices with an Android operating system. The minimum version of Android required is the Gingerbread, Android 2.3.3 API 10. One of the limitations of OpenGL ES 1.0 is that it only renders triangles. To overcome this issue, the COLLADA parser transforms a generic polygon into triangles and recalculates the normal vectors.

There are two ways to render a 3D object (or 2D for that matter) with OpenGL ES 1.0. One is array-based, and the other is element-based. To render the model with the array-based method, the vertices have to be inserted in the right order, so that OpenGL can render them in that sequence. The element-based approach is more flexible, as it does not require changes to the vertices buffer. A pointer to the indices buffer can be manipulated to render certain portions of the model at the time. This allows the program to apply certain attributes, such as color codes, to specific faces of the model without the need to load a complete color buffer with redundant information. The following is the code that renders the 3D model.

3D Model Rendering:

```
public void draw(GL10 gl) {
  //Enable drawing
  gl.glEnableClientState(GL10.GL_VERTEX_ARRAY);
  gl.glEnableClientState(GL10.GL_COLOR_ARRAY);
  gl.glEnableClientState(GL10.GL_NORMAL_ARRAY);
  gl.glFrontFace(GL10.GL_CW);
  gl.glVertexPointer(3, GL10.GL_FLOAT, 0,
                                    vertexBuffer);
  gl.glNormalPointer(GL10.GL_FLOAT, 0,
                                   normalsBuffer);
  int offset = 0;
  for(int i=0; i<materials.length; i++){
    gl.glColor4f(materials[i].rgb[0],
      materials[i].rgb[1],materials[i].rgb[2],
                            materials[i].rgb[3]);
    int length = materials[i].length;
    //!!!!very important
    indexBuffer.position(offset);
    int mode = GL10.GL_TRIANGLES;
    gl.glDrawElements(mode,length*3,
        GL10.GL_UNSIGNED_SHORT,indexBuffer);
    offset += length * 3;
  }
  //!!!!very important
  indexBuffer.position(0);
  //Disable drawing
  gl.glDisableClientState(GL10.GL_VERTEX_ARRAY);
  gl.glDisableClientState(GL10.GL_COLOR_ARRAY);
  gl.glDisableClientState(GL10.GL_NORMAL_ARRAY);
}
```

The application starts by loading the meta-files data of the 3D model previously prepared by the COLLADA parsing program into memory. The 3D model is composed of two parts. One is the upper head, and the other is composed of the mouth and jaws. Combined, they constitute a complete 3D model of a human head. While the application is loading the base model of each part to represent the resting position, a parallel thread is created to load the rest of the meta-files for different expressions. That reduces the startup time to half of what it would be if all the models are loaded in sequence. Once the meta-files are loaded into appropriate arrays and buffers, they are cached using a key-map structure for efficient access.

When there is no input, the application assumes itself to be in an idle situation and starts a timer. The application will periodically monitor the timer, and will randomly replace the resting models with animated ones, creating a frame-based movement effect. As soon as the user enters a text and sends the execute command, the application switches to the speech simulation mode, starts the TTS activity, and synchronizes the mouth animation to create the visual speech effect.

3. LIPS-AUDIO SYNCHRONIZATION

The producer-consumer paradigm[19, 34, 37], a well-studied synchronization problem in Computer Science, is employed to synchronize lip movements with the speech. A classical producer-consumer problem has two threads (one called producer, the other consumer) sharing a common bounded buffer. The producer inserts data into the buffer, and the consumer takes the data out. In our case, the buffer is a queue where characters are entered at the tail and are read at the head. Physically, the queue is a circular queue[19]. Logically, one can imagine it to be a linear infinite queue. The head and tail pointers are always advancing (incrementing) to the right. (To access a buffer location, the pointer is always taken the mod of the physical quenue length, e.g *tail % queue_length.*) If the head pointer catches up with the tail pointer (i.e. *head* = *tail*), the queue is empty, and the consumer must wait. If the difference between *head* and *tail* is equal to the length of the buffer, the queue is full, and the producer must wait.

In the application, the problem is slightly modified: it has one producer and two consumers, each has its own head pointer. The producer is the thread that accepts the input text and puts it in the queue, and the consumers are the Android TTS engine and the animation thread with routine calls to OpenGL ES. The text stream input thread controls the *tail* of the buffer and waits. Every time a new character is entered, *tail* is incremented. The TTS thread and the animation thread read and process the data while each of them is incrementing its own *head*. When the distance between the tail and one of the heads is larger than or equal to a certain empirical constant C, the producer stops and waits for the heads to catch up. When both heads reach for the tail, the producer starts inserting new data into the buffer. To further improve the algorithm, the TTS *head* and the animation *head* wait for each other, which forces the speech and the animation to be more in sync as shown in Figure 5. Below is a Java-like pseudo code for the synchronization of the TTS with the animation using the producer-consumer algorithm.

Producer-Consumer Code:

```
long tail = ttsThread = animationThread =0;
```

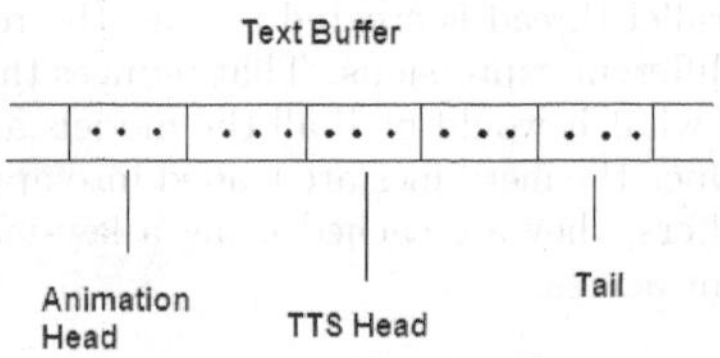

Figure 5: Producer-Consumer Data Buffer

```
//Fixed size buffer
char[] textBuffer = new char[offset];
//Producer thread
while(true){
  if(tail-head1>=offset||tail-head2>=offset)
    inputThread.sleep(100);
  else{
    textBuffer[tail % offset]=ch;
    tail++;
  }
}

//TTS thread
while(true){
  if(head1 == head || head1 >= head2+C1)
  ttsThread.sleep(100);
  else{
    char ch = textBuffer[head1 % offset];
    tts.speak(ch);
    head1++;
  }
}
//Animation thread
while(true){
  if(head2==tail || head2>=head1+C2)
    animationThread.sleep(100);
  else{
    char ch = textBuffer[head2 % offset];
    animation.render(ch);
    head2++;
  }
}
```

4. CONCLUSIONS AND DISCUSSIONS

We have presented the design and implementation of a speech animator for the Android mobile platform using exclusive open-source technologies. A parser written in Java is used to parse a COLLADA file containing 3D model data to a meta-file which can be rendered by OpenGL ES programs. Normally, only the difference between a 3D model and the base model are read from the meta-file. The final model is obtained by overlaying the scene created with the difference data on the base model. The producer-consumer paradigm is used to achieve lips-audio synchronization. The code of the application will be available for students and developers who want to use it as a starting point for further development.

There are unlimited ways of extending and enhancing the application. In particular, it is a significant task to explore the application of the Active Shape Models(ASM) or Active Appearance Model (AAM) developed by Tim Cootes and Chris Taylor in the 1990s[11, 10] to create more realistic 3D models. ASM and AAM are statistical models for image processing, in particular facial recognition. Using ASM or AAM, a system can be trained to generate new sets of data from a reduced covariance matrix and the vector representing the pose model, or the mean shape. In this case, the principal components can be applied to produce the different facial expression by training the model with a sample of visemes, representing the mouth shapes for the different phonemes. That will result in a more realistic movement of the mouth when simulating the visual speech. Some researchers have explored this approach and obtained good results[21].

Another significant enhancement to the application could be an interface enhancement with text messaging feature. Instead of reading the message, the user could listen to it and watch the simulation. It could also be interfaced with a live video streaming application. Instead of transmitting audio and video data which might be huge even after compression, one can transmit only the text of the talking person, along with some control data. The other person can watch and listen to a real-time simulation of the conversation. To realize this, speech recognition capabilities are required at the sender side. The Android platform supports this feature using Google's speech-recognition service[26]. Of course the transmitted text can be compressed by the sender and decompressed by the receiver but no synchronization is needed for the transmitted data as the animation is driven by the text and the lip-speech synchronization is done using the producer-consumer paradigm at the receiver end.

5. ACKNOWLEDGMENTS

We would like to thank Mr. Ted Benic, who helped enhance many of the 3D model images using Blender.

6. REFERENCES

[1] Android Open Source Project: TextToSpeech, *http://developer.android.com/reference/android/speech/*

[2] E. Angel, *Interactive Computer Graphics: A Top-Down Approach Using OpenGL*, Fourth Edition, Addison-Wesley, 2005.

[3] D. Astle and D. Durnil, *OpenGL ES Game Development*, Thomson Course Technology, 2004.

[4] Jun Auza, *The Technology Behind Avatar (Movie)*, *http://www.junauza.com/2010/01/technology-behind-avatar-movie.html*, Jan 2010.

[5] Charles Babcock, *Watson's Jeopardy Win A Victory For Mankind*, Information Week, Feb 2011.

[6] Koray Balc, *Xface: Open source toolkit for creating 3d faces of an embodied conversational agent*, pp. 263-266, Smart Graphics, 2005.

[7] Blender Foundation. Blender.org *http://www.blender.org/*, 2013.

[8] S. R. Buss, *3-D Computer Graphics: A Mathematical Introduction with OpenGL*, Cambridge University Press, 2003.

[9] C. Bregler, M. Covell, and M. Slaney, *Video Rewrite: Driving Visual Speech with Audio*, p.353-360, SIGGRAPH'97 Proceedings, ACM Press, 1997.

[10] T.F. Cootes, G. J. Edwards, and C. J. Taylor, *Active appearance models*, p. 484-498, ECCV, 2, 1998.

[11] T.F. Cootes, C.J. Taylor, D.H. Cooper and J. Graham *Active Shape Models - Their Training and Application*, Computer Vision and Image Understanding, p. 38-59, Vol. 61, No. 1, Jan. 1995.

[12] E. Cosatto, H.P. Graf, and J. Schroeter, *Coarticulation method for audio-visual text-to-speech synthesis*, US Patent 8,078,466, Dec 2011.

[13] P.K. Doenges et al., *MPEG-4: Audio/video and synthetic graphics/audio ifor mixed media*, p.433-463, Signal Processing: Image Communication, ELSEVIER, 9, 1997.

[14] Forbes Magazine, *Android Solidifies Smartphone Market Share*, *http://www.forbes.com/*, Jan., 2013.

[15] Gary C. Martin, *Preston Blair phoneme series*, *http://www.garycmartin.com/mouth_shapes.html*, 2006.

[16] Google Inc. Trimble Navigation Limited. 3D Warehouse. *http://sketchup. google.com/3dwarehouse/*, 2013.

[17] E.R. Harold. *Processing XML with Java: a guide to SAX, DOM, JDOM, JAXP, and TrAX*, Addison-Wesley Professional, 2003.

[18] S. Hill, M. Robart, and E. Tanguy, *Implementing Opengl ES 1.1 over OpenGL ES 2.0*, Consumer Electronics, 2008, ICCE 2008, Digest of Technical Papers, International Conference, IEEE, 2008.

[19] F. June, *An Introduction to Video Compression in C/C++*, Createspace, 2010.

[20] F. June, *An Introduction to 3D Computer Graphics, Stereoscopic Image, and Animation in OpenGL and C/C++*, Createspace, 2011.

[21] G. A. Kalberer, P. Muller, and L.V. Goo, *Modeling and Synthesis of Realistic Visual Speech in 3D*, p. 266-294, 3D Modeling & Animation, edited by N. Sarris and M. G. Strintzis, IRM Press, 2005.

[22] The Khronos Group Inc.,*https://collada.org/*, 2011.

[23] The Khronos Group Inc., *OpenGL ES The Standard for Embedded Accelerated 3D Graphics*, *http://www.khronos.org/opengles/*, 2013.

[24] The Khronos Group Inc., *OpenGL Shading Language*, *http://www.opengl. org/documentation/glsl/*, 2013.

[25] M. Milivojevic, I. Antolovic, and D. Rancic, *Evaluation and Visualization of 3D Models Using Collada Parser and Webgl Technology*, p. 153-158, Proceedings of the 2011 International Conference on Computers and Computing, World Scientific and Engineering Academy and Society (WSEAS), 2011.

[26] S. Mlot, *Google Adds Speech Recognition to Chrome Beta*, *http://www.pcmag.com/article2/0,2817,2414277,00.asp* , PC Magazine, Jan. 2013.

[27] A. Munshi et al., *OpenGL ES 2.0 Programming Guide*, Addison-Wesley Professional, 2008.

[28] I.S. Pandzic and R. Forchheimer, *MPEG-4 Facial Animation:The Standard, Implementation and Applications*, John Wiley & Sons, 2002.

[29] Thomas Rist, and Patrick Brandmeier, *Customizing Graphics for Tiny Displays of Mobile Devices*, p.260-268, Personal and Ubiquitous Computing, 6, 2002.

[30] T. Roosendaal and S. Selleri, *The Official Blender 2.3 guide: free 3D creation suite for modeling, animation, and rendering*, No Starch Press, 2004.

[31] R. J. Rost et al., *OpenGL Shading Language*, Third Edition, Addison-Wesley, 2009.

[32] N. Sarris and M.G. Strintzis, *3D Modeling & Animation*, IRM Press, 2005.

[33] D. Shriener et al., *OpenGL Programming Guide*, Eigth Edition, Addison-Wesley, 2013.

[34] A. Silberschatz et al., *Operating System Concepts*, Addison-Wesley, 1998.

[35] M. Singhal and N.G. Shivaratri, *Advanced Concepts in Operating Systems*, McGraw-Hill, 1994.

[36] Sketchup, *http://www.sketchup.com/intl/en/product/gsu.html*, 2013.

[37] A.S. Tanenbaum, *Modern Operating Systems*, Third Edition, Prentice Hall, 2008.

[38] University of Maryland, *Blendshape Face Animation*, *http://userpages.umbc.edu/bailey/Courses/Tutorials/ ModelNurbsHead/BlendShape.html*, 2009.

[39] L. Wood et al., *Document object model (dom) level 1 specification*, W3C Recommendation, 1, 1998.

[40] T.L. Yu, "Chess Gaming and Graphics using Open-Source Tools", *Proceedings of ICC2009*, p. 253-256, Fullerton, California, IEEE Computer Society Press, April 2-4, 2009.

[41] T.L. Yu, D. Turner, D. Stover, and A. Concepcion, "Incorporating Video in Platform-Independent Video Games Using Open-Source Software", *Proceedings of ICCSIT*, Chengdu, China, July 9-11, IEEE Computer Society Press, 2010.

[42] I. Zbib, *3D Face Animation with OpenGL ES: An Android Application*, CSE Master Project Report, School of Computer Science and Engineering, CSUSB, 2013.

A Pipeline From COLLADA to WebGL for Skeletal Animation

Jeffery McRiffey, Ralph M. Butler, and Chrisila C. Pettey
Computer Science Department, Middle Tennessee State University, Murfreesboro, TN, USA

Abstract - *Effective use of HTML5's canvas and its access to WebGL for rendering 3D content requires knowledge of how to import externally developed 3D content. Additionally, in order to efficiently reuse 3D content in various different browser applications, it is convenient to have a data format that can be rendered directly by the JavaScript program with WebGL. To that end, we have provided a process for extracting data from COLLADA files using Python's elementTree, storing it in a JSON format, and rendering it with JavaScript and WebGL. This process works for skeletal animation as well as other, less complicated, 3D data.*

Keywords: WebGL, COLLADA, Skeletal Animation, Maya, HTML5

1 Introduction

In the past, browser-based 3D graphics have been dependent on cumbersome plug-ins that were deficient in customization, sometimes relied on less efficient software-based rendering, required frequent plug-in related updates, and lacked support for mobile systems [3]. HTML5's canvas and its access to WebGL overcome these deficiencies. However, effective use of these technologies requires knowledge of how to import externally developed 3D content. For static geometry this process is fairly straightforward. The real challenge comes with rendering of skeletal animation. Our goal was to get a 3D object into our existing engine without altering the game engine code so that it could parse 3D files. To do this we decided to develop an external utility that would create an intermediate file using the JSON format. This would allow us to keep the game engine small, and at the same time allow us to investigate what data needed to be extracted. There are several file formats for 3D objects (e.g., dae, fbx, and obj). Since dae seemed to be an industry standard, we started with that. However, the interpretations of the standard were inconsistent (for example we could not move dae files between Blender and Maya). Since the standard was hard to interpret, we looked for software to help us. Surprisingly, at the time we began this, all the software that existed only dealt with static geometry. There were some packages that could understand animations – for instance Maya can import a dae file – but for the most part these were proprietary and did not export the file in a format that we could use.

In this paper we show how the power of Python's *elementTree* can be used to extract skeletal animation data from a COLLADA file converting it to a JSON format that can be rendered by WebGL. We begin with a discussion of the data that is needed by showing an example JSON file. We then show where the data can be found in a COLLADA file and how it can be extracted with Python's *elementTree*. We end with an explanation of how to render the JSON data with JavaScript and WebGL. Figures 1 and 2 show examples of screenshots of skeletal animation done with the process described in this paper. However, these two examples contain more triangles and joints than can be easily described here. Therefore, we will use the example shown in Figure 3 of a cube with nine joints where joints 3 and 4 are animated.

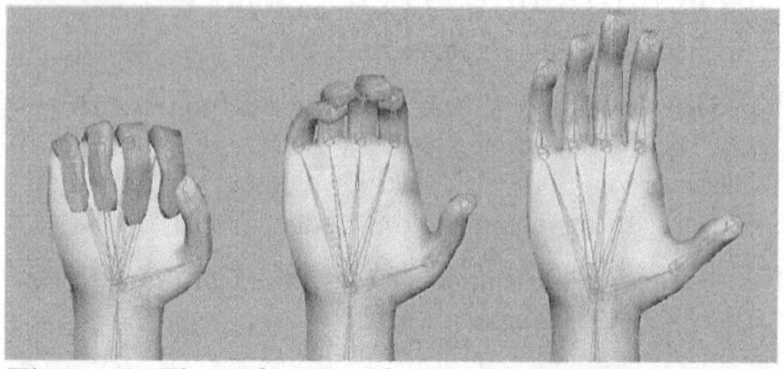

Figure 1. Three frames of a hand opening animation

Figure 2. Three frames of a human jumping animation

Figure 3. Three frames of an animated cube

2 Required data in JSON format

The JSON format is a text based standard used for efficient information serialization and transmission [8]. Specifically, JSON is space efficient and eliminates the need for parsing COLLADA files within the rendering engine. The organization of the final JSON file is a series of key-value pairs. Figure 4 shows a subset of the JSON file for the animated cube shown in Figure 3.

All 3D models have vertices that have positions, normals, and texture coordinates. The three attributes POSITION, NORMAL, and TEXCOORD can be seen as keys in Figure 4. The actual floating point values for the vertex attributes are stored in large arrays (represented as the values [...] in Figure 4). Since each vertex has three values for position, three values for normal, and two values for texture coordinate, each vertex has eight numbers associated with it. Additionally all meshes are ultimately represented as triangles because that is currently required by WebGL. Since a vertex can belong to multiple triangles, the triangles are represented by an array of indices (another key-value pair with INDEX as the key).

The key-value pairs directly related to animation are: JOINT_ID (a list of the joint names), WEIGHT (a list of joints that affect each vertex), BIND_SHAPE_MATRIX (a 4x4 matrix that allows for the mesh to be transformed by the skeleton's coordinate system [2]), JOINT (a description of each joint including the joint's id, parent, and the two 4X4 bind pose and inverse bind pose matrices), and ANIMATION (a dictionary containing a 4X4 matrix for each frame for each joint).

3 COLLADA

COLLADA is an open, XML-based 3D asset format maintained by the Khronos Group [5]. There are a few comments that need to be made about creating the COLLADA files. First, all geometry should be triangulated before exporting because WebGL requires it [3]. Second, all animations should be baked before exporting as COLLADA. Finally, it is necessary to export the transformations as a single matrix (i.e., scale, rotation, and translation information is a single 4X4 matrix for all transformed portions of the model).

To produce the appropriate JSON file we need to scan a COLLADA file for tags that define the elements associated with the JSON keys that were described in the preceding section. This sounds like an easy task, however COLLADA files are typically very large and the data for a single element is scattered throughout the tree hierarchy, sometimes with logical pointers from one portion of the tree into another. In the remainder of this section we will briefly describe the location of the various necessary elements within a Maya generated dae file. While all 3D content packages do produce dae files that conform to the standard, they do not typically produce the same dae file. So we concentrated on dae files produced by Maya.

```
model = {
 "Cube":
 {
  "POSITION": […],
  "NORMAL": […],
  "TEXCOORD": […],
  "WEIGHT": […],
  "JOINT_ID": […],
  "INDEX": […],
  "BIND_SHAPE_MATRIX": […],
  "IMAGE_LOCATION": "textures/box.jpg",
  "JOINT":
  {
   "joint1": {"ID": 0 ,"PARENT": -1,"BIND_POSE":
       […],"INVERSE_BIND_POSE": […]},
   "joint2": {"ID": 1 ,"PARENT": "joint1","BIND_POSE":
       […],"INVERSE_BIND_POSE": […]},
   ...

   "joint8": {"ID": 7 ,"PARENT": "joint1","BIND_POSE":
       […],"INVERSE_BIND_POSE": […]},
   "joint9": {"ID": 8 ,"PARENT": "joint1","BIND_POSE":
       […],"INVERSE_BIND_POSE": […]}
  },
  "ANIMATION":
  {
   "FRAME_LENGTH": 24,
   "FRAMES":
   {
    "joint3":
    {
     1: […], 2: […], 3: […], 4: […], 5: […], 6: […],
     ...
     19: […],20: […],21: […],22: […],23: […],24: […]
    },
    "joint4":
    {
     1: […], 2: […], 3: […], 4: […], 5: […], 6: […],
     ...
     19: […],20: […],21: […],22: […],23: […],24: […]
    },
   }
  }
 }
}
```

Figure 4. Animated cube JSON model file

3.1 Static geometry

The elements related to vertices, positions, normals, texture coordinates, and indices are located within the <library_geometries> element. Arnaud and Barnes [2] mention that the <library_geometries> element may contain numerous <geometry> elements. Furthermore, each <geometry> element includes a <mesh> element. The <mesh> element is the most interesting, as it holds one or more <source> elements and exactly one <vertices> element [2].

Once a <mesh> element is discovered, it must be examined for <source> elements. A typical <source> element will contain a <float_array> and a <technique_common> element. The <float_array> element's content contains a great deal of relevant data, and the <technique_common> element will hold <accessor> information for clarification. The <float_array> *count* attribute discloses the number of values within the array. Since a <mesh> may contain more than one

<source> element, the <source> *id* attribute must be checked against the <input> children of the appropriate parent element.

As an example of the fact that the data for a single element is scattered throughout the COLLADA tree hierarchy, sometimes with logical pointers from one portion of the tree into another, the parent element for position is the <vertices> element, and it is necessary to compare the *source* attribute of the <input> child of <vertices> that has a *semantic* attribute equivalent to “POSITION” with the *id* attribute from the proposed <source> element. If the two attributes match, then the <source> element actually does contain vertex position information. For normals and texture coordinates, the <source> *id* attribute must be matched to an <input> *source* attribute within <triangles> instead of <vertices>.

The <triangles> element links to the texture value for the texture coordinates with its *material* attribute, and the actual indices are stored within the <p> child of the <triangles> element. An <input> child of the <triangles> element with a “VERTEX” *semantic* requires an extra step, as its *source* attribute points back to the <vertices> element. The <input> child of the <vertices> element will be the final reference to the positions array. The *offset* attributes give starting points for each <input> element’s indices.

3.2 Skeletal animation data

Skeletal animation data can be divided into three major parts: joints, weights, and animation frames. The joint names are located within the <library_controllers> element. The <library_controllers> element will contain one or more <controller> elements with a <skin> element. Each joint needs an inverse bind matrix to correctly represent its location [5]. The inverse bind matrices can be extracted from the same <skin> element that contains joint names. The <joints> element should be searched for an <input> with a *semantic* attribute of “INV_BIND_MATRIX.” This <input> *source* attribute points to a <source> that contains a <float_array> element. The <float_array> contains 16 times the number of joints, which represents a 4x4 matrix for each joint. The information in <float_array> will ultimately be stored as separate 4x4 matrices for each joint.

An initial transformation for each joint and a skeleton hierarchy must be determined. Within the <library_visual_scenes> element, a <visual_scene> element will represent joint information as a <node> with a *type* attribute of “JOINT.” The *id* attribute of each found joint should match a name in the relevant <Name_array> element. The first joint <node> found will be considered a root joint, which means the joint has no parent and is not influenced by other joints. Every joint found may have <node> children with “JOINT” *types*. Any child joint <node> will have the current parent <node> as its skeleton parent. Each joint <node> should also contain a <matrix> element. The <matrix> element represents a 4x4 initial transformation matrix. Figure 5 depicts a skeleton hierarchy for the cube in Figure 3 where “joint1” is the parent of 8 other joints.

```
<?xml version="1.0" encoding="utf-8"?>
<COLLADA xmlns="..." version="...">
 <asset>...</asset>
  <library_visual_scenes>
   <node name="joint1" id="joint1" type="JOINT">
    <matrix>...</matrix>
    <node name="joint2" id="joint2" type="JOINT">
     <matrix>...</matrix>
    </node>
    ...
    </node>
    <node name="joint9" id="joint9" type="JOINT">
     <matrix>...</matrix>
    </node>
   </node>
  </library_visual_scenes>
 <scene>...</scene>
</COLLADA>
```

Figure 5. Joint hierarchy and initial transformation matrices

```
<?xml version="1.0" encoding="utf-8"?>
<COLLADA xmlns="..." version="...">
 <asset>...</asset>
  <library_controllers>
   <bind_shape_matrix>
    1.000000 -0.000000 0.000000 -0.053133
    0.000000 1.000000 -0.000000  1.536980
    0.000000 0.000000  1.000000  0.459493
    0.000000 0.000000  0.000000  1.000000
   </bind_shape_matrix>
     <source id="cubeController-Joints">
        <Name_array id="cubeController-Joints-array" count="9">
         joint1 joint2 joint3 joint4 joint5 joint6 joint7 joint8 joint9
        </Name_array>
     </source>
   <source id="CubeController-Weights">
    <float_array id="CubeController-Weights-array"
       count="17">
     1.000000 0.499967 0.499967 0.499975 0.499975 0.499984
     0.499984 0.499990 0.499990 0.499990 0.499990 0.499995
       0.499995 0.499976 0.499976 0.499983 0.499983
    </float_array>
   </source>
   <vertex_weights count="8">
    <input semantic="JOINT" offset="0"
        source="#CubeController-Joints"/>
    <input semantic="WEIGHT" offset="1"
        source="#CubeController-Weights"/>
    <vcount>2 2 2 2 2 2 2 2</vcount>
    <v>
       0 1 4 2     //vertex 0
       0 3 8 4     //vertex 1
       0 5 3 6       //vertex 2
       0 7 7 8       //vertex 3
       0 9 2 10      //vertex 4
       0 11 1 12     //vertex 5
       0 13 6 14     //vertex 6
       0 15 5 16     //vertex 7
    </v>
   </vertex_weights>
  </library_controllers>
 <scene>...</scene>
</COLLADA>
```

Figure 6. Weights and bind shape matrix

Inside the same <controller> element that contains joint information, weight information can also be found. First, a <bind_shape_matrix> element contains a 4x4 matrix that allows for the mesh to be transformed by the skeleton's coordinate system [2]. Next, a single <vertex_weights> contains <input> elements labeled with the *semantic* attributes "JOINT" and "WEIGHT." The *source* attribute of the "JOINT" <input> should match the *source* attribute associated with the corresponding joint names, while the "WEIGHT" <input> points to a new <source> element. That <source> has a <float_array> child that contains all possible weights for the skin. Figure 6 shows the weight information for the skinned animated cube.

All information for animation frames is located in the <library_animations> element. This element contains an <animation> element for each animated joint. The *name* attribute for each <animation> ties it to a specific joint. There is an <input> for a <sampler> for each <animation> that has an "OUTPUT" *semantic* attribute with a *source* attribute that points to a <source> element containing animation transform matrices. That <source> element contains a <float_array> with a *count* attribute equal to 16 times the number of frames since there are 16 elements in each frame matrix. Figure 7 shows a <library_animations> element for "joint3" with all but the first two frames (32 elements) of the float arrays removed for readability. The joint "joint3" is animated for 24 frames in this example, so there are 384 values total.

```
<?xml version="1.0" encoding="utf-8"?>
<COLLADA xmlns="..." version="...">
 <asset>...</asset>
  <library_animations>
   <animation id="joint3-anim" name="joint3">
    <animation>
     <source id="joint3-animation-output-transform">
      <float_array id="joint3-Matrix-animation-output-
        transform-array" count="384">
        0.076020 -0.813660 -0.576349 1.625169
        -0.852682 -0.352678 0.385424 2.151170
        -0.516870 0.462142 -0.720604 -4.021905
        0.000000 0.000000 0.000000 1.000000
        0.076020 -0.813660 -0.576349 1.641187
        -0.852682 -0.352678 0.385424 2.153707
        -0.516870 0.462142 -0.720604 -4.033360
        0.000000 0.000000 0.000000 1.000000
        ...
      </float_array>
     </source>
     <sampler id="joint3-animation-transform">
      <input semantic="OUTPUT" source="#joint3-animation-
        output-transform" />
     </sampler>
    </animation>
   </animation>
  </library_animations>
 <scene>...</scene>
</COLLADA>
```

Figure 7. Animation frame data for "joint3"

4 Python for COLLADA to JSON

elementTree is a Python wrapper that allows the programmer to load XML files and store them as trees of elements. These trees can then be easily searched for the needed information. Figure 8 shows four examples of the simplicity and power of *elementTree*. The *find* method returns the first child of the current element, while *findall* returns all direct children of the current element. Using / specifies the path to the descendant element of the current element, while []'s can be used to specify attributes. For example #1 in Figure 8 will find the first <input> child of the <triangles> child of the current <mesh> that has a semantic attribute of VERTEX. A // can be used to search the entire subtree of the current element. For example #2 in Figure 8 will find all <node>'s that are descendants of <visualScene> while example #3 will find all <nodes>'s of type JOINT that are descendants of <visualScene>. Example #4 will return the first <material> descendant of the <library_materials> child of <root> that has an id of materialName.

```
1. vertexPosSrc =
     mesh.find("./triangles/input[@semantic='VERTEX']")
2. allNodes = visualScene.findall(".//node")
3. jointNodes = visualScene.findall(".//node[@type='JOINT']")
4. material = root.find("./library_materials//material[@id='%s']"
     % (materialName) )
```

Figure 8. Sample *elementTree* code for extracting data from XML

After the data has been extracted, it may have to be massaged in up to three different ways. First, each matrix extracted from the COLLADA file must be converted from row-major to column-major order.

Second, since WebGL can only utilize a single index array, the separate position, normal, and texcoord arrays from the COLLADA file must be altered [3][7]. This index mapping for positions, normals, and texcoords works by examining inline indices in groups of three. For example, if the first indices examined were 3, 0, and 3, then the three elements in the third row of the COLLADA position array should be written to the JSON position array, the three elements in row 0 of the normal array should be written to the JSON normal array, and the two elements of the texcoord array found in row 3 should be written to the JSON texcoord array. The final index for all of these values is now stored as 0. This method is continued with increasing final indices until a repeating group of three original indices is encountered.

Third, each vertex can have zero to n direct joint influences, so weight padding is required. Since WebGL will read a single weight array sequentially, zero weights must be appended to all vertices until they are associated with n weights. In our example n = 3.

5 WebGL

There are four major steps for rendering a JSON model: initializing the WebGL context, compiling the shader program, pushing content from JSON to the GPU, and finally starting the rendering loop. In this paper we will not discuss initializing the WebGL context or the rendering loop as they are basic techniques described in [3] that are independent of what you might be rendering. The other two steps described in this section build on techniques written by Rowell [9], Thomas [11], and Seidelin [10]. Rowell's base code was augmented to support skeletal animation [9].

5.1 Shader program

WebGL uses a subset of the OpenGL Shading Language for rendering known as GLSL ES [3]. Cantor and Jones [3] explain that GLSL ES is a lightweight, C-like language with specialized facilities for handling vectors and matrices. A shader program, consisting of a vertex and fragment shader, is required for rendering [1]. Anyuru [1] goes on to mention that a vertex shader handles geometric data one vertex at a time. The resulting information is converted to fragments and passed to the fragment shader; each fragment has the potential to ultimately become a pixel on the screen [1].

A major goal of this project was to support skeletal animation and basic lighting, which requires more complex shaders. New attributes for normals, joint identifiers, and joint weights must be sent to the vertex shader. Additionally, each vertex uses extra uniforms for all joint transform matrices, a normal matrix, and lighting information. A new varying variable for light weighting is also passed to the fragment shader. Figure 9 shows a commented and extensively altered fragment of a vertex shader for skeletal animation and lighting.

5.2 JSON to GPU

Once the shader program has been initialized, data can be accessed from the JSON model and sent to the shaders. First the *IMAGE_LOCATION* is used to a load the texture image; the image must finish loading before any information is pushed to the GPU (Figure 10 shows how to initialize a texture). Next the *POSITION*, *NORMAL*, *TEXTCOORD*, *JOINT_ID*, *WEIGHT*, and *INDEX* arrays from the JSON model must be put into buffers for the vertex shader (see Figure 11). After the texture has loaded and the buffers have been filled, they can be pushed to the GPU. This requires setting up a vertex attribute pointer and binding each buffer [9] (Figure 12). The final step before drawing the scene is setting the uniforms based on the current projection, model-view, normal, and joint matrices (Figure 13).

The projection, model-view, and lighting uniforms only need to be updated when the perspective changes, the camera moves, or the model is transformed, so they do not need to be updated for every frame. Since the joint matrices are meant for animation, they have the potential to change for each frame and should be handled differently than the other uniforms.

To calculate the joint matrices, a float array of size 16 times the maximum number of joints should be populated with JSON data. Every joint has a name, parent name, bind matrix, and inverse bind matrix in the JSON file. Since a joint can influence other joints, a set of world joint transformations must be calculated. A joint's world matrix is equal to the product of its parent's world matrix and its own bind pose matrix; if a joint has no parent, its world matrix is simply its own bind pose matrix. A joint's world matrix is then multiplied by its inverse bind matrix and the skin's bind shape matrix. The resulting 4x4 matrix can then be stored before being sent to the shader. If the model has associated animations, then the current frame's joint matrix takes the place of the joint's bind pose matrix for world matrix calculation. Figure 14 gives pseudocode for calculating the skinning and animation matrices for joints.

```
attribute vec3 aVertexPosition;   //positions x,y,z
attribute vec3 aVertexNormal;     //normals x,y,z
attribute vec3 aJointID;          //joint ids padded to 3
attribute vec3 aJointWeight;      //joint weights padded to 3
uniform mat4 uJMatrix[30];        //up to 30 4x4 joint matrices
uniform mat4 uMVMatrix;           //4x4 model-view matrix
uniform mat4 uPMatrix;            //4x4 projection matrix
uniform vec3 uLightingDirection;  //light direction
void main(void)
{
   vec4 newVertex; //vertex after joint transformations
   vec4 newNormal; //normal after joint transformations
   //if no joint influences still render the vertex
   else
   {
      //calculate the new vertex based on the corresponding joint matrices
      newVertex = uJMatrix[int(aJointID[0])] *
            vec4(aVertexPosition, 1.0) * aJointWeight[0];
      newVertex = uJMatrix[int(aJointID[1])] *
            vec4(aVertexPosition, 1.0) * aJointWeight[1] + newVertex;
      newVertex = uJMatrix[int(aJointID[2])] *
            vec4(aVertexPosition, 1.0) * aJointWeight[2] + newVertex;
      newVertex[3] = 1.0;
      //calculate the new normal based on the corresponding joint matrices
      newNormal = uJMatrix[int(aJointID[0])] *
            vec4(aVertexNormal, 0.0)  * aJointWeight[0];
      newNormal = uJMatrix[int(aJointID[1])] *
            vec4(aVertexNormal, 0.0)  * aJointWeight[1] + newNormal;
      newNormal = uJMatrix[int(aJointID[2])] *
            vec4(aVertexNormal, 0.0)  * aJointWeight[2] + newNormal;
   }
//calculate final vertex position
   gl_Position = uPMatrix * uMVMatrix * newVertex;
//send textcoords to frag shader
//if no lighting, send frag weights of 1.0
//else
   //calculate final normal from the normal matrix and xyz
   //coordinates of newNormal
   //set dirLightWeighting to the dot product of
   //transformedNormal and uLightingDirection or 0.0, return the
   //largest value
   //calculate light weighting and send to frag shader
}
```

Figure 9. Vertex shader for skeletal animation and lighting

6 Conclusions and future work

The work presented here provides a brief overview of a process for extracting the 3D skeletal animation content from a COLLADA file generated by Maya, summarizing that data in a JSON file, and rendering the JSON data with JavaScript and WebGL. The topic for this work was specifically chosen due to a lack of applicable literature on the process. It should be noted that due to the length requirements for the paper, it is impossible to give a detailed description of the entire process. Interested readers can get a more detailed description by checking out the the subversion directory (svn co http://svn.cs.mtsu.edu/svn/vw3/trunk vw3). The *thesis* directory contains a detailed description of the process. The *dae2json.py* files are in the *utils* directory. A short tutorial and demo are located at http://vw3.cs.mtsu.edu.

While the COLLADA files used in this work were generated from Maya, we believe that the Python program would work with COLLADA files generated from other 3D content development packages such as Blender. This would provide us with a stable pipeline for extracting 3D data from any existing COLLADA file for rendering in any HTML5/WebGL browser application without altering the browser application.

```
//The following algorithm is from [11]
//creat a texture, and image, and load the image
var objectTexture = glContext.createTexture();
objectTexture.image = new Image();
objectTexture.image.src = model['cube']['IMAGE_LOCATION'];
objectTexture.image.onload = function () //wait for image to load
{
  //set the texture as the current texture
  glContext.bindTexture(glContext.TEXTURE_2D, objectTexture);
  //flip the data along the vertical axis
  glContext.pixelStorei(glContext.UNPACK_FLIP_Y_WEBGL, true);
  //upload the image to the GPU
  glContext.texImage2D(glContext.TEXTURE_2D, 0, glContext.RGBA,
      glContext.RGBA, glContext.UNSIGNED_BYTE,
      objectTexture.image);
  //fast image scaling up close
  glContext.texParameteri(glContext.TEXTURE_2D,
      glContext.TEXTURE_MAG_FILTER, glContext.NEAREST);
  //fast image scaling far away
  glContext.texParameteri(glContext.TEXTURE_2D,
      glContext.TEXTURE_MIN_FILTER, glContext.NEAREST);
  //set current texture to null so the previous texture
  //isn't accidentally altered
  glContext.bindTexture(glContext.TEXTURE_2D, null);
}
```

Figure 10. Texture initialization

```
//function createArrayBuffer(values) and function
//createElementArrayBuffer(values) come from
//Rowell's class [10]
var objectBuffers = {};
//Create the position buffer
objectBuffers.positionBuffer =
    createArrayBuffer(model['cube']['POSITION']);
//Similar calls for normal, texture, joint weight, and joint id buffers
    ...
//Finally create the element array buffer for indices
objectBuffers.indexBuffer =
    createElementArrayBuffer(model['cube']['INDEX']);
```

Figure 11. Creating data buffers

```
//push index buffer and bind the buffer
glContext.bindBuffer(glContext.ELEMENT_ARRAY_BUFFER,
    objectBuffers.indexBuffer);
//push position buffer,
//bind the buffer and set the vertex attribute pointer
glContext.bindBuffer(glContext.ARRAY_BUFFER,
    objectBuffers.positionBuffer);
glContext.vertexAttribPointer(
    shaderProgram.vertexPositionAttribute,
    3, glContext.FLOAT, false, 0, 0);
//normals,joint ids, joint weights are all bound in the same manner
//as positions the code has been omitted to save space
//texture buffer is bound like the other data
glContext.bindBuffer(glContext.ARRAY_BUFFER,
    objectBuffers.textureBuffer);
glContext.vertexAttribPointer(shaderProgram.textureCoordAttribute,
    2, glContext.FLOAT, false, 0, 0);
//activate current texture, bind it, and send it to the frag shader
glContext.activeTexture(glContext.TEXTURE0);
glContext.bindTexture(glContext.TEXTURE_2D, texture);
glContext.uniform1i(shaderProgram.samplerUniform, 0);
```

Figure 12. Sending attributes to the vertex shader

```
//set up pMatrix
var view = 45; //vertical field of view
var aspectRatio = glContext.viewportWidth / glContext.viewportHeight;
var minDist = 1;
var maxDist = 500;
var pMatrix = mat4.create(); //empty 4x4 matrix
mat4.perspective(view, aspectRatio, minDist, maxDist, pMatrix);
//set up mvMatrix
var mvMatrix = mat4.create();        //empty 4x4 matrix
mat4.idenity(mvMatrix);              //no transforms yet
mat4.translate(mvMatrix, [1, -5, -10]); //trans mvMatrix for x, y, z
mat4.rotate(mvMatrix, .75, [0, 1, 0]); //rotate 0.75 radians for y
mat4.rotate(mvMatrix, .25, [1, 0, 0]); //rotate 0.25 radians for x
var lighting = true;                 //turn lighting on or off
var lightingDirection = [-0.3, -0.3, -1.0]; //set lighting direction
var lightingColor = [0.1, 0.1, 0.1]; //set ambient lighting color rgb
var directionalColor = [0.9, 0.9, 0.9]; //set directional lighting rgb
//normalize lighting direction
var ald = vec3.create();
vec3.normalize(lightingDirection, ald);
vec3.scale(ald, -1);
if(lighting)
{
  //enable lighting and pass ambient lighting color to shader
  glContext.uniform1(shaderProgram.useLightingUniform, true);
  glContext.uniform3fv(shaderProgram.ambientColorUniform,
        lightingColor);
  //similarly pass directional lighting color and direction to the shader
}
//pass pMatrix to the shader as mat4
glContext.uniformMatrix4fv(shaderProgram.pMatrixUniform,
    false, pMatrix);
//similarly pass mvMatrix
//create and pass a normal matrix for proper lighting
var normalMatrix = mat3.create();
mat4.toInverseMat3(mvMatrix, normalMatrix);
mat3.transpose(normalMatrix);
glContext.uniformMatrix3fv(shaderProgram.nMatrixUniform,
    false, normalMatrix);
```

Figure 13. Sending uniforms to the shaders

```
function setUniformJointMatrix
{
  for(each joint)
  {
    store parent name;
    set world_matrix to an empty 4x4 matrix;
    if(animation frame exists)
    {
      if(not a root joint)
        set world_matrix to parent_world_matrix * frame_matrix;
      else
        set world_matrix to frame_matrix;
    }
    else
    {
      if(not a root joint)
        set world_matrix to parent_world_matrix * bind_pose_matrix;
      else
        set world_matrix to bind_pose_matrix;
    }
    set new_matrix to world_matrix * inverse_bind_pose_matrix;
    set final_matrix to bind_shape_matrix * new_matrix;
    store final_matrix;
  }
  send all matrices to the shader;
}
```

Figure 14. Psuedocode for calculating joint matrices

7 References

[1] Anyuru, A. 2012. *Professional WebGL Programming: Developing 3D Graphics for the Web*. Wrox, Chichester, UK.

[2] Arnaud, R., and Barnes, M. 2006. *COLLADA: Sailing the Gulf of 3D Digital Content Creation*. A K Peters, Wellesley, MA.

[3] Cantor, D., and Jones, B. 2012. *WebGL Beginner's Guide*. Packt, Birmingham, UK.

[4] Irish, P., Möller E., and Zijdel, T. 2012. requestAnimationFrame for Smart Animating. http://paulirish.com/2011/requestanimationframe-for-smart-animating/, Oct. 2012

[5] Khronos, 2012, COLLADA 3D Asset Exchange Schema. https://www.khronos.org/collada, Sept. 2012.

[6] Khronos, 2012. WebGL Specification. https://www.khronos.org/registry/webgl/specs/latest, Sept. 2012.

[7] Milivojec, M., Antolovic, I., and Rancic, D. 2011. Evaluation and Visualization of 3D Models Using COLLADA Parser and WebGL Technology. In *International Conference on Computers and Computing* (Lanzarote, Canary Islands, Spain, May 2011), 153-158.

[8] Mozilla, 2012. JavaScript Reference. https://developer.mozilla.org/en-US/docs/JavaScript/Reference, Sept. 2012.

[9] Rowell, E. 2011. *HTML5 Canvas Cookbook*. Packt, Birmingham, UK.

[10] Seidelin, J. 2012. *HTML5 Games: Creating Fun with HTML5, CSS3, and WebGL*. John Wiley and Sons. Chichester, UK.

[11] Thomas, G. Learning WebGL. http://www.learningwebgl.com/blog, Sept. 2012.

SESSION

VIRTUAL REALITY + COMPUTER GRAPHICS + RELATED METHODS

Chair(s)

TBA

Plasma Visualization in Parallel using Particle Systems on Graphical Processing Units

T.S. Lyes and K.A. Hawick
Computer Science, Massey University, North Shore 102-904, Auckland, New Zealand
email: {t.s.lyes, k.a.hawick}@massey.ac.nz
Tel: +64 9 414 0800 Fax: +64 9 441 8181

April 2013

ABSTRACT

Visualising and simulating charged plasma systems present additional challenges to conventional particle methods. Plasmas exhibit multi scale phenomena that often prevent the use of standard localisation approximations. Plasmas as particle systems that emit light are important in many interesting components of games, computer animated movies such as weapons fire, explosions, astronomical effects. They also have intrinsic value for simulating physical phenomena. We describe the use of various shader and texture methods to render a simulated plasma system based on explicitly charged particles. We report on attainable renderings and on coding approaches and performance using graphical processing units.

KEY WORDS
plasma simulation; special effects; particles; electrostatic charge; rendering.

1 Introduction

Plasmas present additional challenges for their simulation and visualization over and above those normally associated with particle systems. The key physics characteristic of a plasma is that it is an ionized gas [1]. Ionization can occur by applying extreme heat, pressure or electric discharge (such as a strong magnetic field). Plasma contained charged particles called ions; these can be either positively or negatively charged. This makes plasma strongly responsive to electromagnetic fields and electrically conductive. Such properties make plasma different to those of solid, liquid and gaseous states of matter. Our sun is an example of a large plasma system, but closer to earth the Aurora Borealis, ionosphere and neon signs are all examples of plasmas. Plasma physics is also an important part of fusion energy research [2].

Plasma simulation is often described as multi-scale or multi-level. This refers to the fact that plasma systems behave on a wide range of different lengths and time scales [3] [4]. This makes plasma systems difficult to simulate when trying to include all the relevant physics, thus, approximate models are used with trade-offs between accuracy and computational efficiency. A number of localisation approximations are commion place in molecular dynamical simulations [5], but teh multiple scales in plasma systems generally require a different simulation approach.

There are two main approaches to computational modeling of plasma systems - a fluid approach and a kinetic (particle) approach. Fluid approaches such as hydrodynamics or magnetohydrodynamics (MHD) are the most popular, but are inaccurate when more detailed kinetic processes (for example, particle interactions) affect the behaviour of the plasma. Kinetic simulation approaches can model plasma over larger ranges of density and temperature [6] and are more accurate, but are computationally expensive [7]. One way of dealing with this issue is the use of hybrid modeling techniques featuring elements of both fluid and particle systems which compromise between computational effectiveness and result precision [7].

The Particle-in-Cell (PIC) approach is an example of a kinetic approach to plasma simulation [8, 9]. Other well known kinetic methods include the Vlasov and Fokker-Planck methods [4]. Object-oriented methods of the Particle-in-Cell approach have proven successful in modeling plasma systems to a good degree of accuracy while also minimizing performance issues. VORPAL [10] is a plasma simulation code designed using an object-oriented style of PIC (OOPIC), while [2] investigates methods of parallelizing OOPIC systems in a variety of different programming languages. Other models treat plasma as a 6-dimensional phase-fluid [6], which are more complex than typical MHD models. Kinetic modeling has also been used in the simulation of interactions between plasma and pulse laser systems [11], and particle-based methods have been successful in simulating plasma systems relating to the motion of blood cells [12].

In graphics, plasma simulations can be a eye-catching edition to any video game or movie. In these situations, accuracy of physics can be approximated further as the plasma systems need only to appear to behave correctly. However, the problem still remains of simulating a system which is accurate (visually) while also being computationally expensive. Parallelizing the behaviour of the plasma system can significantly improve the computational performance of the system. Graphics Processing Units (GPUs) [13] are excellent devices for simulating highly-parallel systems such as particles [14].

This paper uses a particle-based plasma system to simulate a ball of plasma. It uses NVidia's Compute Unified Device Architecture (CUDA) [15] to parallelize the plasma code and inter-operate with OpenGL [16] to render the system in real time using a variety of rendering techniques. In Section 2 the core functionality of the plasma system is described and the main equations explained. Section 3 gives the results of the simulation, showing the different rendering techniques used. Section 4 presents a discussion of the performance of the program on two different GPU graphics cards as well as using different rendering setups, and performance statistics are presented in a variety of tables. Finally Section 5 concludes the project and offers some ideas on future work in the area.

2 Simulation Method

Our primary objective in this present article is to present the visual rendering approaches for charged plasma systems. We therefore do not dwell on time-integration algorithms and other simulation details such as finite differencing algorithms [17], but we do however summarise the main features that differentiate plasma simulations from other *ad hoc* potential particle simulations.

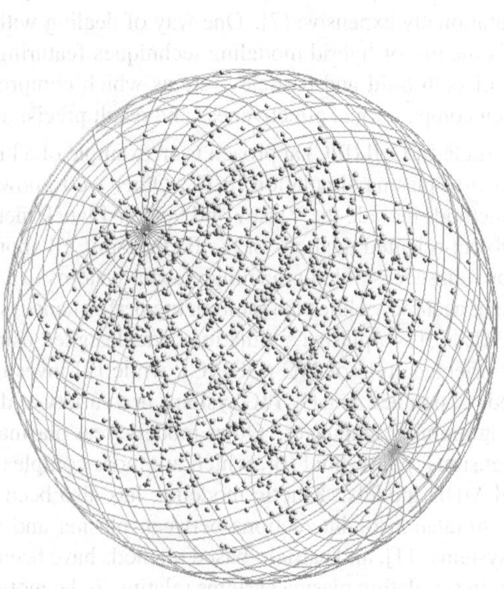

Figure 1: A spherical shell is used to contain the particles used to simulate the plasma body.

A plasma system can be simulated by using a particle system. Particles in the system represent the positive ions and negative electrons making up the plasma. A positive charge will attract a negative charge, while both positive or negative charges will repel each other. In this particular system, the plasma is contained in a bounding sphere as shown in Figure 1. Without some sort of container, a plasma system does not have a particular shape but just spreads as the ionized gas that it is.

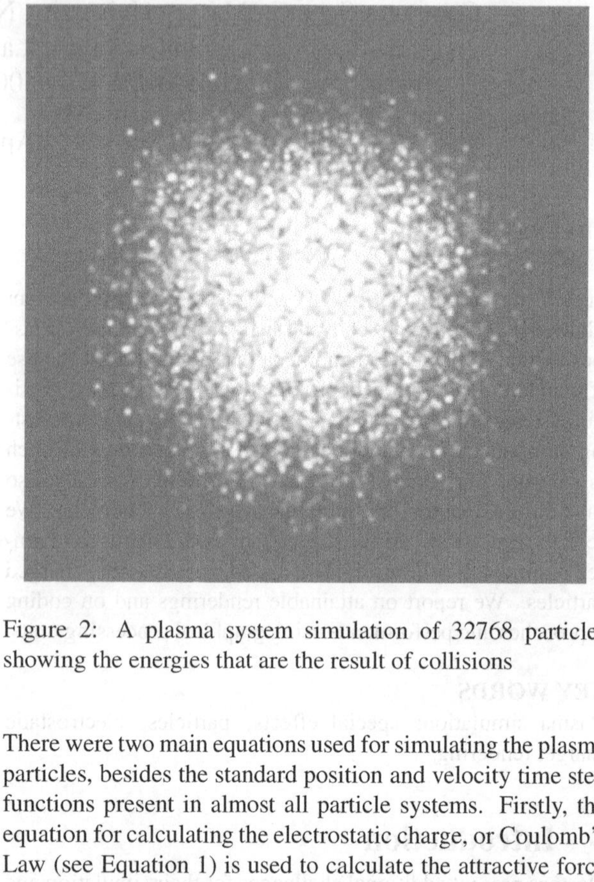

Figure 2: A plasma system simulation of 32768 particles showing the energies that are the result of collisions

There were two main equations used for simulating the plasma particles, besides the standard position and velocity time step functions present in almost all particle systems. Firstly, the equation for calculating the electrostatic charge, or Coulomb's Law (see Equation 1) is used to calculate the attractive force between any two particles at one time. For simulation purposes, constants such as ϵ had to be altered slightly such that the system was able to be observed in real time. In any case, the equation implies the electrostatic force is determined primarily on the distance r between the two particles in question (a smaller distance means a stronger force), while the charges of the two particles determine whether the force will attract or repel the particles.

$$F_{i,j} = q_i q_j / 4\pi\epsilon_0 r_{i,j}^2 \quad (1)$$

Secondly, the energy of each particle is given by the formula in Equation 2, which is the equation for kinetic energy of a particle. For the purpose of the simulation, it can be assumed that all particles in the system are the same mass. Additionally, no external forces (including gravity) are applied to the system during the simulation. The total energy of the system must remain constant, so the potential energy of each particle is converted into kinetic energy during collisions and attractions, and this change in kinetic energy can be used to colour the simulation - a faster moving particle will be brighter than a slower moving one.

$$E_k = \frac{1}{2}mv^2 \tag{2}$$

The particular particle system used to model the plasma in this paper had several important properties. Firstly, unlike some other particle systems, particles in the plasma system cannot be created or destroyed beyond the initialization of the system . This is essential for maintaining some degree of equilibrium in the system and makes sure the particles do not break free from the confining boundaries. Secondly, particles positions and velocities are known and updated every time step of the simulation, and an attraction force is applied to each particle depending on its own electric charge in relation to other particles around it. The simulation is not treated as being run in a vacuum - therefore, some damping force is applied every time step. This is a trivial aspect to the simulation, as if we were to simulation a plasma system such as the Sun, such a system does occur in a vacuum (space). This particular system is contained with a spherical boundary. Particles colliding with the boundary are bounced back into the system with some damping force applied as well. Finally, particles are coloured depending on the rendering method used in the simulation.

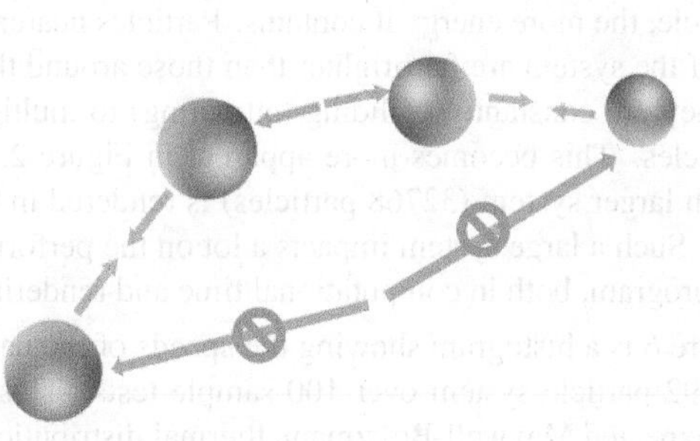

Figure 3: Example interactions between different particles in the plasma system

Figure 3 shows some example interactions between particles in the plasma system. The blue and grey spheres represent the different charged particles. There are three main situations that arise; firstly, particles of opposite charge are attracted to one another. Secondly, particles with the same charge are repelled away from each other. The third situation occurs between particles large distances apart; although normally the blue particles would repel each other, in this particular system they do not affect each other because they are too far away. Typically this would involve each particle belonging to a different non-neighbouring cell in the system, thus when computing collisions between neighboring cells, the interaction would never be established. This occurs for both attracting particles and repelling particles.

As with most particle systems, the system requires a large amount of particles for it to believably resemble a real plasma system. This can become problematic when requiring calculations of energy and charge between each and every particle in the system, resulting in often hundreds of millions of computations (order N-squared) every time step of the simulation. This issue can be solved by parallelizing parts of the system using CUDA. The update functions for each particle can be parallelized and run simultaneously, but the largest speedup in performance may come from using CUDA to sort the particle arrays in such a way that they need not communicate with every particle in the system when checking for collisions - only the particles within some area of the current particle need to be checked. While this sorting functionality does require additional time to sort the arrays, it makes up for this by dramatically decreasing the execution time of the collision checking functions. Specifically for this system, three main CUDA kernels were used; one for updating position and velocity arrays, one for sorting the arrays, and one for handling collisions between the particles. A generic overview of the algorithm used to update the plasma system is shown in Algorithm 1.

Algorithm 1 A general plasma system update algorithm

```
for all timestep do
    calculate position hash table
    sort particles
    calculate cells
    for all particles in cell do
        calculate collisions
    end for
    for all particles in system do
        update positions, velocities
    end for
end for
```

Further performance improvements can be made using the interoperability functionality with CUDA and OpenGL [15]. This involves using vertex buffer objects (VBOs) to store data and render it directly on the graphics card , thus avoiding the overhead of copying the data to and from the device every time step. This particular simulation keeps both the positions and colours of the particles in VBOs, using a vertex array and colour array respectively. The velocity of the particle does not need to be kept in a VBO as it is not a visual aspect of the simulation, rather, a behavioural aspect. However, the velocity is still taken into account when rendering the particles based on the energy output - the colour of the particles is determined primarily on their velocity, so this will be used to populate the colour VBO.

Figure 4: A plasma system simulation showing the positively (white) and negatively (blue) charged particles

The simulation was run using a series of different rendering methods to observe the performance changes in each. Firstly, the system was rendered using texturing, with the billboarding technique used similar to [18]. This method did not make use of the OpenGL-CUDA interoperability. The particles were coloured according to the charge of the particle - white if positive, and blue if negatively charged. A second rendering method used the particles calculated energy to colour the particles. Additionally, two shaders [19, 20] were used to render the system, one a spherical shader with depth perception, and one a sprite shader with blending. All simulations were run on a NVidia Quadro 4000 GPU and also on a newer GeForce GTX 680

3 Performance Results

A range of system sizes were tested for the simulation. Frame rates were monitored and displayed on screen in real time and were also averaged over several thousand iterations for each rendering technique used. Comparisons were made between the different techniques regarding both their visual and computational performance.

Figure 4 shows the plasma system rendered using non-VBO texturing and the billboarding technique. This system size was 8192 particles - this system size was found to produce an acceptable level of frames per second for the texture rendering. The particles are coloured according to the charge of the particle - white if the charge is positive, and blue if the charge is negative. It is mainly used to demonstrate the distribution of charge throughout the entire system. During the initialization phase of the simulation particles are assigned a random charge value, irrespective of the particles position in the system.

Figure 5: A plasma system simulation rendering the particles showing the energies that are the result of collisions

Using a similar method, Figure 5 renders the plasma system as textures but this time they are coloured according to the energy of the particles from the collisions. The brighter the particle, the more energy it contains. Particles nearer the center of the system are far brighter than those around the edges, as they are constantly colliding (attracting) to multiple other particles. This becomes more apparent in Figure 2, where a much larger system (32768 particles) is rendered in the same way. Such a large system impacts a lot on the performance of the program, both in computational time and rendering time.

Figure 6 is a histogram showing the speeds of the particles of a 8192 particle system over 100 sample tests. This exhibits the expected Maxwell-Boltzmann thermal distribution.

Figure 7 shows the plasma system rendered using a spherical shader and VBOs to take advantage of CUDA-OpenGL interoperability. Using spheres it is easier to gauge the exact positions of individual particles due to the depth perception that is enabled as well as the particles not needing to be blended, however it does not look particularly realistic compared to other simulations. It is worth noting that spherical shaders produced the fastest frames per second results of all the rendering techniques tested.

A different shader was used in the simulation shown in Figure 8. The results are similar to those shown in Figures 4 and 4, despite being rendered using VBOs. While the average frame rate of the simulation while using this rendering technique is similar to other techniques, when the system is moved further away from the camera the FPS greatly increases (in

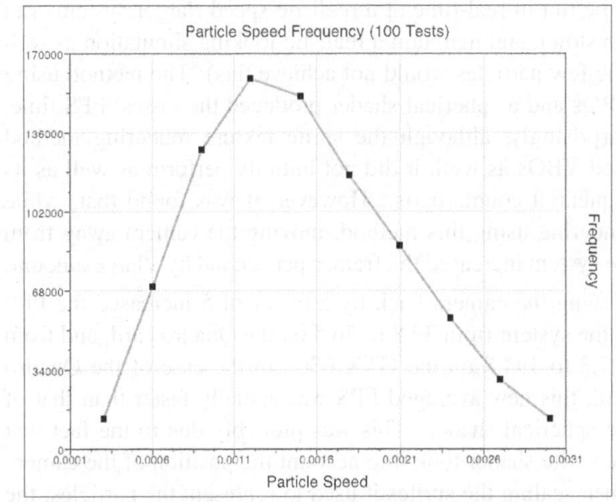

Figure 6: Graph showing the velocity distribution of particles over some frames

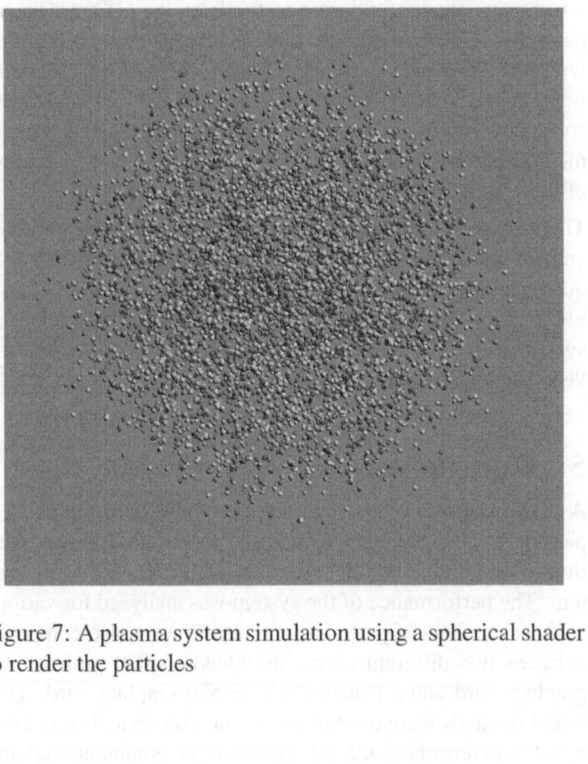

Figure 7: A plasma system simulation using a spherical shader to render the particles

Figure 8: A plasma system simulation using a texture shader to render the particles

other methods, this does not happen). This suggests this rendering technique would be best suited for rendering objects which are far away (for example, a sun in the sky) to get the best results.

4 Discussion

Performance was monitored by timing the kernel execution and averaging it over 10,000 executions. The mean execution times were taken for both cards and used to show the comparison between the Quadro card and the newer GeForce graphics card. The three kernels were not timed individually. Additionally, performance regarding the graphical frame rate was also monitored to observe the performance differences between the different rendering methods. Frame rates were displayed in real time as the simulation was run, as well calculating a mean frame rate over 10,000 executions. Statistics were collected for four system sizes; 4096, 8192, 16384 and 65536 particles.

No. of Particles	time(Quadro) seconds	time(GTX 680) seconds
4096	0.0064	0.00348
8192	0.0153	0.00581
16384	0.0491	0.01406
65536	0.6541	0.14542

Table 1: Average kernel execution times for a plasma system of various sizes

Firstly, it is important to note that the system speeds up the further the particles drift apart - this is because the particles will not need to perform the attraction collision functions as often if they are spread out, as there are less particles in the immediate vicinity and surrounding cells. When the simulation is first started, the particles are not distributed evenly within the bounding sphere - rather, they are distributed closer to the center, and gradually expand outwards as the simulation progresses. The times observed will therefore be slower than expected from a system in an almost equilibrium state, however they are more closely representative of an active plasma system which is constantly moving, which is also a more realistic system.

Table 1 shows the average execution times for all kernels for each particle system size, tested for both the Quadro 4000 card and the GeForce GTX 680 card. It can be shown that the execution times of the kernels increase exponentially as the size of the system increases. The render method used was the spherical shader method.

No. of Particles	Avg FR Quadro frames / sec	Avg. FR GTX 680 frames / sec
4096	188.4	332.5
8192	73.6	205.7
16384	21.2	87.4
65536	1.4	6.9

Table 2: Average frame rates of a particle system of different sizes

Table 2 compares the frame rates observed for various plasma system sizes using both the Quadro and GTX 680 graphics cards. As mentioned earlier, the system speeds up as particles spread out, when there are less collisions per cell. This effects the average frame rate as well. Because they are averaged over this time frame, the observed FPS in tables 2 and 3 will be faster than when the system is first initialized, and slower than when the system has reached an almost equilibrium state. It was found that the optimum system size for the Quadro card was the 8192 particle system size, however the newer GTX 680 could easily render the system 16834 particle system.

Render Method	FR Quadro seconds	FR GTX 680 seconds
Textures	40.2	64.5
Energy	40.6	63.7
Sphere VBO	73.6	205.7
Sprite VBO	39.8	107.3

Table 3: Average frame rates of a 8192 particle system using different rendering methods.

Table 3 shows the average frame rates observed when using each rendering method. The simulation was restricted to run only using a system size of 8192 particles, as from previous tests it was decided that this system size gave the best result for the Quadro card, considering the simulation needed to be run in real-time at a realistic speed (larger systems run too slow), and maintain a realistic looking simulation as well (too few particles would not achieve this). The method using VBOs and a spherical shader produced the fastest FPS time. Surprisingly, although the sprite texture rendering method used VBOs as well, it did not initially perform as well as its sequential counterparts. However, it was found that, while rendering using this method, moving the camera away from the system increased the frames per second by a large amount.

Moving the camera back by a factor of 5 increased the FPS of the system from 39.8 to 76.5 on the Quadro card, and from 107.3 to 194.8 on the GTX 680. In the case of the Quadro card, this new averaged FPS was actually faster than that of the spherical shader. This was probably due to the fact that the sprite shader took into account the position of the camera when scaling the sprites it used to represent the particles; the closer the camera, the larger the sprites would need to appear, and thus the more pixels were needed to render. Interestingly enough, none of the other rendering methods (including the spherical shader) got FPS increases when moving the camera back. As mentioned previously, this observation suggests that the sprite pixel shader would be an ideal method to use when rendering objects that would need to appear far away (such as a sun on the horizon or in space).

What was also noticeable was the substantial increase in speed when using shader rendering methods on the GTX 680 compared to the other methods. Specifically, using the GTX 680 with textures resulted in an increase in FPS of 60.4 percent, while VBO spheres increased by 179.5 percent and VBO sprites by 169.6 percent. This suggests that these rendering methods are better designed for parallelization and up-scaling of the system in general.

There is scope to incorporate stereo rendering of the particles and plasma cloud more generally. The framerates are adequate and therefore with additional GPU hardware it is feasible to attain the necessary framerate doubliong to render the system in stereo [21, 22]. This has the potential to aid the visualisation considerably.

5 Conclusion

A plasma system of charged particles was simulated using a particle system. OpenGL was used to visualize the simulation in real time, and CUDA was used to parallelize the system. The performance of the system was analyzed for various sizes or numbers of particles, and results were also compared between two different cards, the Quadro 4000 professional graphics card and a newer GeForce 580 graphics card. Different methods were used to render the plasma and were evaluated to determine trade-offs between the computational and visual performance of the system. These methods included using VBOs and shaders to render the plasma.

A texture shader or sprite shader gave the best results visually, while the spherical shader resulted in the faster frame rates. The sprite shader, while initially having the slowest rendering speed, performed better when the camera was further away from the system, and this was not the case for the other rendering techniques. When rendering this particular plasma system on the Quadro card, it was found that a system size of 8192 particles was best when considering both the computational performance and visual aspects of the system. The GeForce GTX 680 card could handle a system size of at least 16384 particles in real time, however a system size of 65536 particles could not be rendered in real time by either card.

There is scope to extend this work. Writing new shaders specifically designed for representing a plasma system could result in great improvements to the simulation both computationally and visually. With regards to the behavioural mechanics of the system, the current simulation does not deal whatsoever with electromagnetic fields or fluxes. Plasma systems are known to respond strongly to electromagnetic fields and simulating this would be quite interesting. For example, having points on the bounding sphere acting as electric field points or introducing an electric field in some other way might lead to some interesting behaviour from the plasma system, such as the creation of beams or other complex behavior such as a sun's corona.

References

[1] Bellan, P.M.: Fundamentals of Plasma Physics. Cambridge (2006)

[2] Norton, C.D., Szymanski, B.K., Decyk, V.K.: Object-oriented parallel computation for plasma simulation. Communications of the ACM **38** (1995) 88–100

[3] Park, W., Belova, E.V., Fu, G.Y., Tang, X.Z., Strauss, H.R., Sugiyama, L.E.: Plasma simulation studies using multilevel physics models. Physics of Plasmas **6 (5)** (1999) 1796 – 1803

[4] Sugiyama, T., Kusano, K.: Multi-scale plasma simulation by the interlocking of magnetohydrodynamic model and particle-in-cell kinetic models. Journal of Computational Physics **227** (2007) 1340 – 1352

[5] Allen, M., Tildesley, D.: Computer simulation of liquids. Clarendon Press (1987)

[6] Gibbon, P., Berberich, R.S.B., Karmakar, A., Arnold, L., Masek, M.: Plasma simulation with parallel kinetic particle codes. In: NIC Symposium. (2010)

[7] Bartos, P., Blazek, J.: Hybrid computer simulation scheme for computational study of low-temperature plasma containing micrometer-sized dust particles. IEEE Transactions on Plasma Science **38, No 9** (2010) 2407 – 2411

[8] Markidis, S., Lapenta, G., Rizwan-uddin: Multi-scale simulations of plasma with ipic3d. Mathematics and Computers in Simulation **80** (2010) 1509 – 1519

[9] Liewer, P.C., Decyk, V., Dawson, J., Fox, G.C.: A universal concurrent algorithm for plasma particle-in-cell simulation codes. In: Proc. Third Hypercube Conference. Number C3P-362 (1988) 1101–1107

[10] Nieter, C., Cary, J.R.: Vorpal: a versatile plasma simulation code. Journal of Computational Physics **196** (2004) 448 – 473

[11] Kemp, A.J., Cohen, B.I., Divol, L.: Integrated kinetic simulation of laser-plasma interactions, fast-electron generation and transport in fast ignition. Physics of Plasmas **17 (5)** (2010) 1 – 7

[12] Tusubota, K., Wada, S., Yamaguchi, T.: Particle method for computer simulation of red blood cell motion in blood flows. Computer Methods and Programs in Biomedicine **83** (2006) 139 – 146

[13] Leist, A., Playne, D.P., Hawick, K.A.: Exploiting Graphical Processing Units for Data-Parallel Scientific Applications. Concurrency and Computation: Practice and Experience **21** (2009) 2400–2437 CSTN-065.

[14] Hawick, K.A., Playne, D.P., Johnson, M.G.B.: Numerical precision and benchmarking very-high-order integration of particle dynamics on gpu accelerators. In: Proc. International Conference on Computer Design (CDES'11). Number CDE4469, Las Vegas, USA, CSREA (2011) 83–89

[15] NVIDIA® Corporation: CUDA™ 3.1 Programming Guide. (2010) Last accessed September 2010.

[16] Woo, M., Neider, J., Davis, T., Shreiner, D.: OpenGL Programming Guide: The Official Guide to Learning OpenGL. 3rd edition edn. Addison-Wesley (1999) ISBN:0201604582.

[17] Playne, D.P., Hawick, K.A.: Comparison of GPU Architectures for Asynchronous Communication with Finite-Differencing Applications. Concurrency and Computation: Practice and Experience (CCPE) **Online** (2011) 1–11

[18] Lyes, T.S., Hawick, K.A.: Fire and flame simulation using particle systems and cuda. Technical Report CSTN-168, Computer Science, Massey University, Albany, North Shore 102-904, Auckland, New Zealand (2012)

[19] Bailey, M., Cunningham, S.: Graphics Shaders - Theory and Practice. Second edn. CRC Press (2012) ISBN 978-1-56881-434-6.

[20] Engel, W., ed.: SHADER X3 - Advanced Rendering with DirectX and OpenGL. Charles River Media (2005)

[21] Lyes, T.S.: Review of stereo vision. Technical Report CSTN-155, Computer Science, Massey University, Albany, North Shore 102-904, Auckland, New Zealand (2011) In Proc. IIMS Postgraduate Student Conference, October 2011.

[22] Lyes, T., Hawick, K.: Implementing stereo vision of gpu-accelerated scientific simulations using commodity hardware. In: Proc. International Conference on Computer Graphics and Virtual Reality (CGVR'11). Number CGV4047, Las Vegas, USA, CSREA (2011) 76–82

The Component Entity System for Virtual Environments

Justin Ehrlich
School of Computer Sciences, Western Illinois University
Macomb, Illinois, US

Abstract - *This paper reviews a novel design pattern, named Component Entity System (CES), which has become popular for developing commercial and independent games. While the CES pattern is popular within game development communities, it has yet to be formally introduced to the virtual reality academic field. Traditionally object oriented design patterns have been used to develop games, and while this works well for simple environments, it soon becomes unmanageable due to a proliferation of classes, duplicate code, and over-customization of a complex environment. The beauty of the CES design pattern is the separation of functionality from entities. Entities are little more than a collection of functional components that can change dynamically during runtime, all managed by systems. It's an elegant design pattern that should be used as a basis for any large environment architecture. An open-sourced example was created as an example of an architecture utilizing CES.*

Keywords: virtual reality, design pattern, component entity system, game

1 Introduction

In the past few decades virtual reality has become a "holy grail" across a multitude of disciplines. It has been researched and used as a tool for education[1], interventions for special education[2][3], trainers for the military and government[4], and even improving cognition[5]. Programming virtual environments is a massive undertaking that can quickly overwhelm even the best programmers due to the exponential growth of complexity as environment entities that interact with each other and their environment increase. When developing complex interactive environments, it is imperative to choose a good design pattern that allows for extensibility and modulation without introducing a rigid architecture that is too complex to efficiently actually use. Also, it's important to design the architecture in such a way that a non-technical designer can add content to the environment at run-time via a script, without having to program the changes and recompile. This allows the development of an environment to be divided between the design and programming portions. Also, if developed carefully, others outside of development team should be able to extend the environment for other purposes.

1.1 Object Oriented Past

Virtual environments are data-driven in that entities, environments, and events are allowed to enter the system and asynchronously interact with each other. An almost infinite number of possible situations are possible at any moment and interaction between entities and their environments depend on these conditions. The modularity of the entities and the interactions between these entities dynamically change in the environment and may not, and should not, be known at compile time, which makes strict object oriented programming inconvenient and unmanageable. Classic inheritance does not work well as a design pattern for large virtual environments. Typically these environments contain entities, environments, and managers that keep track of each. A general manager might keep of all of the entities, so there is usually a base class named Entity. A render manager might keep track of all of the entities that can be rendered, so Entity may be subclassed as DrawableEntity. Further, some of these entities can move, so are subclassed to a MoveableDrawableEntity object, so a physics manager can keep track of them. Some of the objects move differently, so ones that can fly may be subclassed as FlyableMovableDrawableEntity. Every time more functionality is added, the hierarchy is increased. This eventually causes a proliferation of subclasses that can become unmanageable. Further, as functionality is added a choice must be made of adding to the root or to the leaves of the hierarchy. If added to the leaves, duplication of code will be inevitable, e.g., multiple physics methods that do the same thing may be added to a rock and a brick subclass. If added to the root, there will be functionality in objects that shouldn't have it, e.g., a rock can jump. This anti-pattern is identified by West [6] as the "blob."

A better approach is to use composition as opposed to inheritance. This gives two important benefits: runtime composition of entities and the removal of an unruly hierarchy of classes. To compose an entity at runtime, instantiated functionality can be added dynamically. For instance, there may be a pointer to a *move* object that defines the movement functionality. Initially an object may be controlled by an artificial intelligence object. If this was a flyable object, than an instance of the *ComputerFlyMove* class may be passed to the object and pointed to by the *move* pointer. Some other time the user may want to take control of the object. The *ComputerFlyMove* object can be replaced by the *UserMove* object anytime. By breaking up the functionality into individual classes, the functionality of the object can be defined and redefined at runtime without having to compile specialized classes. There only needs to be functional class pointers and accessor methods that support this dynamic change. As noted by West [6], the disadvantage is that a "blob" still exist. Without inheritance, it will be necessary to have pointers to objects for every possible type of functionality possible in an entity. A rock may have null in place of the move pointer.

A better solution is to remove these pointers and instead define each entity as a collection of functional component objects. This design pattern, named Component Entity System (CES), is an excellent approach for developers to use when developing complex virtual environments because it solves most of the traditional Object Oriented Programming (OOP) patterns in existence. While the CES pattern is popular within game development communities [7][8], it has yet to be formally introduced to the Virtual Reality academic field. As a note, there have been design patterns introduced that are similar, such as Pettifer, Cook, Marsh and West's DIVA3 [9]. I have recently been using the CES design pattern for my advanced graphics courses and research projects (virtual reality-based interventions for those with Autism) and it has proven to be popular among my students and research colleagues. It's important to formalize design patterns to not only make the designing and development phase of a project more efficient, but to also improve team collaboration. If a common design pattern is used, it's easier for others to extend the work since the architecture is already somewhat understood. I created a simple arcade shooting game named *Alien Invasion* to demonstrate the CES design pattern. It is written in C# and targets the XNA 4.0 framework. The source is licensed under the Simplified BSD License and is available here: https://www.assembla.com/code/ComponentEntitySystemAlienInvasion/git/nodes or using git: git://git.assembla.com/ComponentEntitySystemAlienInvasion.git. I'll be taking examples from the code to demonstrate the rest of this paper.

2 A Better Approach: Component Entity System Architecture

In order to permit the functionality of entities to dynamically change at runtime, composition over inheritance is a must. For entities to be given additional functionality, new pointers must be added to the *Entity* class creating a proliferation of pointers to objects that encapsulate functionality. A better approach is to use one base class for all functionality and have the entities keep track of all this functionality in a collection. This allows developers to extend the functionality of a virtual environment without modifying the entity class, which so modifications should not break any other code. By allowing an unrestricted collection of components, an entity can be made up of any combination of components at runtime without re-compiling. A designer can create a new entity type without programming or compiling. By only debugging the various components, the programmers do not need to worry about every possible combination, therefore the debugging stage much is much less complicated and timely.

2.1 Component

The components encapsulate the functionality of the entities. In order to allow any combination of components and to assure encapsulation of functionality, the components are autonomous and do not know about each other. This autonomous organization allows the system to be extended or modified without worrying about side effects, which can cause problems that are difficult to debug. There is no direct message passing, although indirect exchanges of information are done by the systems, which is discussed further in the system section. The entity class will keep track of a collection of components, but will not be concerned with which types. Therefore there must be one base type that is an interface for all other components. As an example of how minimal this component should be defined, figure 1 demonstrates the simplicity of the component interface from my *Alien Invasion* game.

```
public abstract class IComponent
{
}
```

Figure 1: The Component Interface

The data is also encapsulated so each component manages its own function and data. Therefore each component does not need to know about its entity to which it belongs. As an example, an entity may require a position component. Any data that is necessary for the functionality should be contained within the component. While this may tempt a programmer to create large components, it's not advisable because this may cause duplication of code and data, e.g., both a moving component and a static component keep track of the entity's positions. Typically complex functionality can be broken into multiple components and any messaging will be handled by the system. For instance, the moving component can be broken down into both a velocity and a position component. The position component only keeps track of the position while the velocity keeps track of velocity and perhaps acceleration. A moveable entity will contain both of these components while a static entity will only contain the position. As will be discussed later, this will also allow only one system to manage these components instead of two. This system will update the position component with the velocity calculated by the velocity component. The velocity component is demonstrated in figure 2.

```
class VelocityComponent : IComponent
{
    public Vector2 Velocity { get; set; }
    public Vector2 Acceleration { get; set; }
    public VelocityComponent(Entity entity,
        Vector2 velocity, Vector2 acceleration)
    {
        Velocity = velocity;
        Acceleration = acceleration;
    }
    public void Update(GameTime gameTime)
    {
        Velocity = Velocity + Acceleration
            * (float)gameTime.ElapsedGameTime.TotalSeconds;
    }
}
```

Figure 2: The Velocity Component

2.2 Entity

Each entity is defined by an "is-a" relationship to its components, so the entity class defines a collection of components and accessor methods to interface to this collection. Since all of the functionality and data is encapsulated in the components, there is no need to place any other fields besides an identification number to allow for communication between systems. As explained earlier, there should be no subclassing of entities since any added functionality is placed in components. Therefore my entity class, as shown in figure 3, is a sealed class.

```
sealed public class Entity
{
    public int ID { get; private set; }

    private List<IComponent> components;

    public Entity(int ID)
    {
        this.ID = ID;
        components = new List<IComponent>();
    }

    public T GetComponent<T>()where T : IComponent
    {
        if (HasComponent<T>())
            return components.OfType<T>().First();
        else
            return null;
    }

    public bool HasComponent<T>() where T : IComponent
    {
        return (components.OfType<T>().Count() > 0);
    }

    public void AddComponent<T>(IComponent component) where T : IComponent
    {

        if (!HasComponent<T>())
        {
            components.Add(component);
        }
    }
}
```

Figure 3: Entity Class

The components are stored in a list of type IComponent and can be retrieved by the subclass of the IComponent. For instance, if the velocity manager needed to retrieve the velocity component from a specific entity, it could call tempEntity.GetComponent<VelocityComponent>(). In this simplistic implementation, if there are more than one components of the same type only the first is retrieved. There may be times where multiple component types need to be supported, such as an entity storing two different resources of the same type. In this case the GetComponent will need to return a list containing these components, e.g., components.OfType<ResourceComponent>().

2.3 System

Systems are where the entities and components are managed. In its most basic form, and as implemented in *Alien Invasion*, all of the systems are composed and managed within a system manager. The system manager also keeps track of all of the entities through a single list. In typical interactive environments, the application, or "game," loop first retrieves information from the user, updates the game entities, and renders the scene [10]. In a CES system, the application loop does the same thing, but through a collection of systems. During the application loop all of the systems are called to update the list of entities. Each manager goes through the list and determines if the entities contain the valid components for its operation. As Wenderlich [11] explains, this process is analogous to a lock and key. For instance, in order for an entity to unlock the move system, the move system checks the teeth of the key for both the velocity and position components. Both of these must be there because there will be indirect communication between them. If the move system verifies these two components exist, then the velocity is updated by calling update along with the amount of time that has passed since the last call. Then the new velocity is sent to the update method of the position component to update its position. Refer to figure 2 for the details. The lock allows for an entity to dynamically lose or gain functionality without breaking the system. If a moveable objects becomes unmovable, e.g. an entity dies, the move system will simply not update the entity. The first system to be called is the user system, which updates all entities that contain a *UserMoveComponent*, which contains the necessary functionality to interact with the user. This system may also require the velocity component, as the velocity component receives a new velocity based upon the user controls.

The last system to be called in the application loop is the *draw* system. The *Alien Invasion's draw* system requires both a position and a drawable component. Since the *Alien Invasion* is a 2D game, all that the drawable component holds is the sprite to draw. The drawable component receives the position from the position component via the draw system, which works similar to the move system. Figure 4 lists the code for the *draw* system. If a programmer decided to render the game in 3D, she could easily do so by only switching out the draw component with one that draws in 3D. Figure 5 is a screenshot taken from *Alien Invasion* demonstrating the 2D game.

```
class DrawSystem : System
{
    public override void Draw(List<Entity> Entities,
        GameTime gameTime, SpriteBatch spriteBatch)
    {
        foreach (Entity entity in Entities)
        {
            if (entity.HasComponent<DrawableComponent>() &&
                entity.HasComponent<PositionComponent>())
            {
                PositionComponent positionIComponent =
                    entity.GetComponent<PositionComponent>();
                entity.GetComponent<DrawableComponent>().Draw(gameTime, spriteBatch,
                    positionIComponent.Position, positionIComponent.Scale);
            }

        }
    }
}
```

Figure 4: The Draw System

3 Conclusions

The Component Entity System is a flexible design pattern that allows for creating a complex virtual environment while maintaining a simple extensible design. The beauty of the CES design pattern is the separation of functionality from entities. Entities are little more than a collection of functional components, managed by systems. An entity is defined by its functionality, and this functionality can change dynamically during runtime. Functionality can be added without breaking existing code. By treating the entity as a collection of functional components, the unmanageable proliferation of classes can be avoided. The code becomes much cleaner and entity functionality can be dynamically altered at run time without writing an entirely new subclass. This allows the code to be extended much easier, and even allows designers to develop entities without ever touching the code. The CES design pattern should be a starting point for developers to avoid the pitfalls of over complex design.

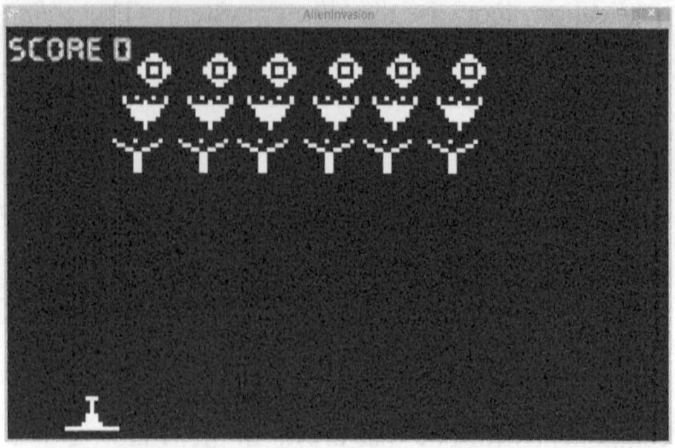

Figure 5: Alien Invasion!

4 Bibliography

[1] E. Ai-Lim Lee, K. W. Wong, and C. C. Fung, "How Does Desktop Virtual Reality Enhance Learning Outcomes? A Structural Equation Modeling Approach," *Computers & Education*, 2010.

[2] S. H. Chen and V. Bernard-Opitz, "Comparison of personal and computer-assisted instruction for children with autism," *Mental Retardation*, vol. 31, p. 368, 1993.

[3] P. Mitchell, S. Parsons, and A. Leonard, "Using Virtual Environments for Teaching Social Understanding to 6 Adolescents with Autistic Spectrum Disorders," *Journal of Autism & Developmental Disorders*, vol. 37, pp. 589–600, 2007.

[4] B. Bergeron, "Developing Serious Games (Game Development Series)," 2006.

[5] L. S. Colzato, P. J. A. van Leeuwen, W. P. M. van den Wildenberg, and B. Hommel, "DOOM'd to switch: superior cognitive flexibility in players of first person shooter games," *Frontiers in Cognition*, vol. 1, 2010.

[6] "Cowboy Programming » Evolve Your Hierarchy." [Online]. Available: http://cowboyprogramming.com/2007/01/05/evolve-your-heirachy/. [Accessed: 15-Mar-2013].

[7] M. Dickheiser, *Game Programming Gems 6 (Book & CD-ROM)*, 1st ed. Charles River Media, 2006.

[8] "Component Based Entity System Design Part 1 - Purple Pwny Studios." [Online]. Available: http://purplepwny.com/blog/component_based_entity_system_design_part_1.html. [Accessed: 17-Mar-2013].

[9] S. Pettifer, J. Cook, J. Marsh, and A. West, "DEVA3: architecture for a large-scale distributed virtual reality system," in *Proceedings of the ACM symposium on Virtual reality software and technology*, New York, NY, USA, 2000, pp. 33–40.

[10] M. Stutz, *The Linux cookbook: tips and techniques for everyday use*. San Francisco: Linux Journal Press, 2001.

[11] "Introduction to Component Based Architecture in Games." [Online]. Available: http://www.raywenderlich.com/24878/introduction-to-component-based-architecture-in-games. [Accessed: 18-Mar-2013].

Data Structures Learning – A Visually Assisted Approach

Loay Alzubaidi[1], Ammar El Hassan[2]

[1]Department of Computer Engineering & Science, Prince Muhammad bin Fahd University
AL-Khobar, Saudi Arabia
lalzubaidi@pmu.edu.sa

[2]Department of Information Technology, Prince Muhammad bin Fahd University
AL-Khobar, Saudi Arabia
aelhassan@pmu.edu.sa

Abstract

Visual aids and multimedia contribute positively to the pedagogical value of in-class and eLearning education. In this paper, we experiment with a visualization tool to gauge its effect on the test scores and, by implication, the understanding levels within Data Structures course offered at Junior level for Computer Science students. Data Structures constitutes an important foundation topic in computer science education which many students fail to do well at due to the complexity of some of its concepts and theories. Therefore, we anticipate that this (Java Applet) tool will support the teaching and help students better understand the (C++) coding and algorithms relating to Binary Search Trees (BST). The test pool is a segregated learning environment which enables us to look at the effect of visual aids on gender as well. The percentage of test score improvement between the group of students who use the visualizer and those who do not ranges between 10 and 13 percent. Although, male students do perform slightly better with the help of the visual aids, the difference in performance does not constitute a major advantage that supports gender related performance theories

Keywords: *Algorithms, Binary Search Tree, Code-Behind, Data Structures, Learning, Pedagogical, Syntax, Visualiser*

1. Introduction

The significance of Algorithms and Data Structures [1, 2 and 4] within Computer Science education is often undermined by the complexities of the concepts and the difficulties in communicating those concepts in an effective way. This is compounded by the position of data structures and algorithms courses on college study plans. As a fundamental subject required by two or three majors within IT colleges, it tends to be offered at sophomore or junior levels. In doing so, we automatically divide the class into two groups based on the level of comprehension achieved. Leaving the course for a further semester or year (to wait for students' technical maturity to improve) has a counter effect on the whole study plan with unacceptable delays. Therefore the solution to the problem of understanding the complexities in data structures and algorithms cannot be legislated for by shifting the position (order) of the course within college study plans; rather it needs to be based on current position of the course within study plans. For such a solution to stand a good chance of success, it needs to additional support in the form of modern education techniques including eLearning applications [4, 7], visualization [6, 10], games [3, 5], web-based, visual interactive programs [7, 9] and animations etc. as a new avenue in the search for the optimum knowledge dissemination technique.

To this end, we introduce in this paper an intelligent visual representation of some of the concepts of data structures. We will show with a Java applet how a typical data structures function such as INSERT is performed both visually and with the corresponding code generated simultaneously and in parallel. The idea is that this can aid the learning process in the classroom with practical visualization that demonstrates the correctness of the theory, thus increasing their motivation and, by implication, understanding as well [11, 12]. In the sections to follow, some of the work carried out on the effects of computer visual aid tools on learning will be introduced, together with the visualizer that was used in this study, this will be followed by the methodology followed and the statistical data collected during study, finally the conclusions and further work will be discussed.

2. Learning with Visual Aids

Some of the work carried out in this area includes an earlier project that utilized the motivational effect of gaming as a learning tool [3, 12]. Although we are not developing a learning game in this paper, it is envisaged that the visualizer tool presented here will contribute to the overall motivation of the students as much as a typical game would. The motivational aspect is only one of the outputs of the learning support system that we are anticipating; other components include gender-specific learning patterns [14], effect of knowledge levels in the course prerequisite, and also the effect of the visualizer on the performance of the students. As we will show with statistical data collected over two consecutive semesters, the visualizer does contribute a notable increase in the performance and, by implication, the understanding of the students. Another notable (and expected) phenomenon is the discrepancy in the increment in performance between the two genders.

3. Methodology & Process

The BST is a Binary tree, which meets the following requirements:

- Each node contains a key
- The key of every node in the left sub-tree is smaller than the key of this node
- the key of every node in the right sub-tree is larger than the key of this node

Previously, students in the Data Structures course performed poorly in the area of BST manipulation (Search, Insert, etc.) due to lack of understanding of:

(i) The complexity of the theoretical concepts presented

(ii) The syntax and logic of the C++ code used to illustrate the ideas

The visualizer created in this research was inspired by similar work in this area [17] and will demonstrate major functionality relating to binary search trees, including Insert (Sequential), Insert (Random), Search and Delete. The node definition for the tree is shown below; noteworthy in the figures that follow in this section is the inclusion of the code-behind feature which shows the syntax of the required function as a statement-by-statement C++ code.

A. Node Definition

```
struct node {
int key;

node* left;

node* right};
```

B. Insert Operation

The Insert operation should follow the binary search tree property.

If the key value to insert is less than the key value of root, new node should be inserted to the left sub-tree. If left sub-tree is null, simply insert the new node here.

If the key value to insert is greater than that of the root, new node should be inserted in the right sub-tree. If right sub-tree is null, simply insert new node here.

Other scenarios are illustrated in the recursive pseudo code below.

```
//////////////////////////////////////////////////////////////////////
// Purpose: insert node with data t into the BST
// Inputs:   pointer of new node , pointer of tree_node
// Effect:   do nothing if tree already contains node
//           otherwise, add the new node
//////////////////////////////////////////////////////////////////////

Insert(new_node * , tree_node * )
if tree_node is not True then
        tree_node ← new_node;
else if (key of new_node < key of tree_node)
        insert(new_node , left child of tree_node)
else
        insert(new_node, right child of tree_node)
endif
```

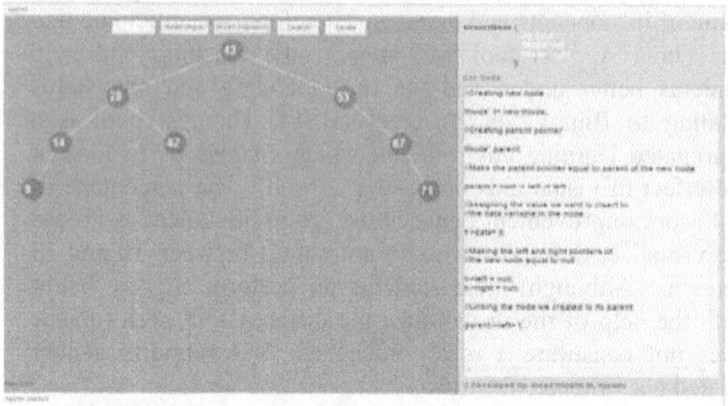

Figure 1. Graph of insert operation with C++ code

Figure 1, Shows the state of the application with a few nodes already inserted. By inserting a new node the application follows the BST property and simple C++ code displayed in the left side of the application to show the students adding process step by step.

C. Search Operation

Searching for a node in a BST is analogous to the Insert operation, above. The search algorithm traverses the tree "in-depth" by following binary search tree property and comparing key values of each visited node with that of the target node.

```
//////////////////////////////////////////////////////////////////////
// Purpose: find Item in the Tree
// Inputs:   target to be found, tree_node pointer
```

```
// Output:   pointer of node containing the target
//           , if it exists; NULL otherwise.
//////////////////////////////////////////////////////////////////////

search (tree_node * , int target)
if (tree_node = NULL)
        return NULL
else if ( target < key of tree_node )
        return search(left child,target)
else if ( target > key of tree_node)
        return search(right child, target)
else
        return tree_node
endif
```

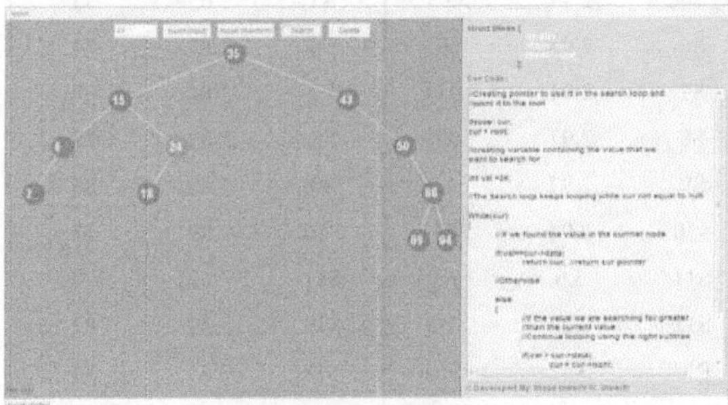

Figure 2. Graph of search operation with C++ code

D. Delete Operation

The Delete operation on binary search tree is more complicated than the Add and Search operations. It is best divided into two stages:

a) search for a target node
b) if the node is found, run specific delete algorithm depending of the node status:

    i. Node is a leaf
    ii. Node has one child
    iii. Node has two children

```
//////////////////////////////////////////////////////////////////////
// Purpose: delete node
// Inputs:   target value to be deleted, tree_node pointer
// Effect:   update binary search tree by deleting the
//           target node
//////////////////////////////////////////////////////////////////////

delete( target , tree_node * )
// use the temp * as temperary pointer
If (target < key of tree_node)
        delete(target, left child)
else if (target > key of tree_node)
        delete(target, right child)
else    // found the node to be deleted! Take action
        //based on number of node children
        if (both children equal NULL)
                delete tree_node
        else if (left child = NULL)
                // node with a right child
                temp = tree_node
                tree_node = righ child of tree_node
                delete temp
        else if (right child = NULL)
                // node with a left child
                temp = tree_node
                tree_node = left child of tree_node
                delete temp
        else    // Removing a node with 2 children
                //SWAP the key of tree_node with the
                //Minimum key from right subtree

                temp = pointer of node with the
                        Min key from right subtree
                key of tree_node = key of temp
                delete(key of temp, right child)
```

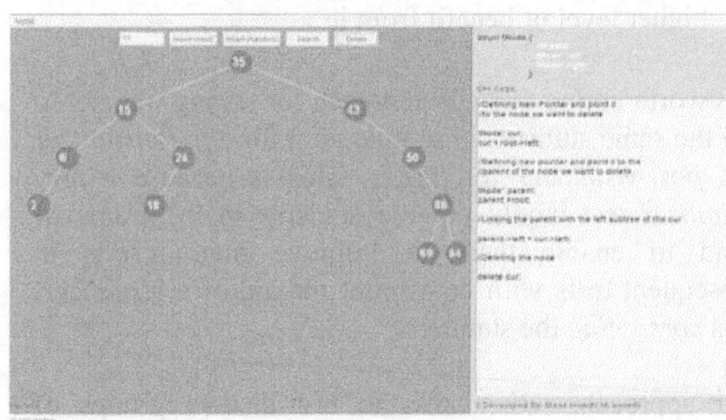

Figure 3. Graph of Delete operation with C++ code

4. Test Statistics

With the assumption that the visualization application will be of positive pedagogical value, we conducted an experiment over a period of two consecutive semesters involving Computer Science students at PMU. The results obtained, in accordance with our expectations do support the original hypothesis of the importance of visual aids for learning plus some unexpected results. The results are discussed in this section. The experiment that was conducted consisted of a Major exam on the subject of Binary Trees; specifically on the main concepts: definition, syntax of node declaration, code for Insert, Search and also Delete. The student samples were selected according to the following criteria:

- 4 samples: 2 Female classes and 2 Male classes.
- 2 samples (1 Female and 1 Male) used the visualization tool and 2 did not
- Sample size is 20 students, distributed evenly around the **Average GPA** for the group: 5 below; 5 equal (roughly) and 5 above average. 5 students from each group had to be eliminated due to various reasons, like missing the exam or having technical difficulties with workstations (including Java support on the host environment) or other technical problems like computer crashes.

Prior to conducting the experiments and collecting the data, our initial set of expectations, based on teaching experience, were as follows:

- All students would benefit from the visual aids as supportive material to the textbook and slides
- The effect of the visual aids would, at worst, be negligible, but most likely, quite positive
- As the visual aid application is gender-neutral [16], Female students would be affected by it in the same way as male students. As Computer Science and IT instructors though, we were anticipating that males would *enjoy* the visualizer more and hence gain a higher level of benefit from it.

It is worth noting that our approach for testing was not to use the same students in sample pool for a *pre-visualizer* and *post-visualizer* test [18]. This is because a *pre-visualizer* test would put the students in the frame of mind to enable them to improve their results in subsequent tests with or without the aid of a *visualizer*, thus *corrupting* the statistics.

Our approach, rather, was to test distinct groups of students taught by the same instructor from the same textbook. We based our grouping criteria on the students GPA within the College of Computer Engineering & Science at PMU. This enabled us to obtain results which are reasonably representative of the effects of the *visualizer* aid. Hence our philosophy is that a student with 2.5 GPA would probably score a similar result to another student with 2.5 GPA if they are both taught by the same instructor and from the same textbook; this is unless one of the two students had a distinct instructional advantage like a *visualizer*.

Due to the fact that we are testing different students in each test group, the effect of the *visualizer* on the performance of the students in the exam cannot be gauged perfectly, there is no elegant solution for this problem unless we can somehow roll-back/wipe the students memory of any exam questions. By the same token, it can be argued that there is a problem of *sample pollution* that takes place when the same student is tested twice in a short time span [18]. Neither approach is perfect, the approach presented here is sufficiently indicative of the phenomenon being studied.

Table 1. Test scores - Male and Female students

Males – No Visualizer			Males – With Visualizer		
ID	**GPA**	**Test Score %**	**ID**	**GPA**	**Test Score %**
S1	2.2	56	S1	2.4	69
S2	2.54	61	S2	2.3	72
S3	2.48	50	S3	2.4	64
S4	2.32	62	S4	2.5	73
S5	2.44	39.5	S5	2.63	55
S6	2.95	60	S6	2.87	74
S7	2.91	41	S7	2.84	69
S8	2.97	69	S8	2.83	77
S9	2.97	64.5	S9	2.88	86
S10	2.94	67	S10	2.89	77
S11	3.6	85	S11	3.62	90
S12	3.22	81.5	S12	3.39	87
S13	3.42	79	S13	3.35	84
S14	3.32	66.5	S14	3.34	83
S15	3.41	87	S15	3.78	92.5
Average	**2.91**	**64.60**	**Average**	**2.93**	**76.83**
Females – No Visualizer			Females – With Visualizer		
ID	**GPA**	**Test Score %**	**ID**	**GPA**	**Test Score %**
S1	2.6	39	S1	2.48	61
S2	2.3	61	S2	2.33	66
S3	2.4	54.5	S3	2.44	60
S4	2.65	43.5	S4	2.23	58
S5	2.65	34	S5	2.62	55
S6	2.89	49.5	S6	2.81	78
S7	2.91	67	S7	2.8	73
S8	2.93	62	S8	2.88	74
S9	2.89	71	S9	2.92	74
S10	2.88	72	S10	2.98	86
S11	3.72	69	S11	3.3	72.5
S12	3.36	83	S12	3.45	84
S13	3.67	76.5	S13	3.12	91
S14	3.57	89	S14	3.33	90
S15	3.61	91	S15	3.47	92
Average	**3.00**	**64.13**	**Average**	**2.88**	**74.3**

The test results are listed in table 1 above, showing Student ID, GPA and Test Score Percentage.

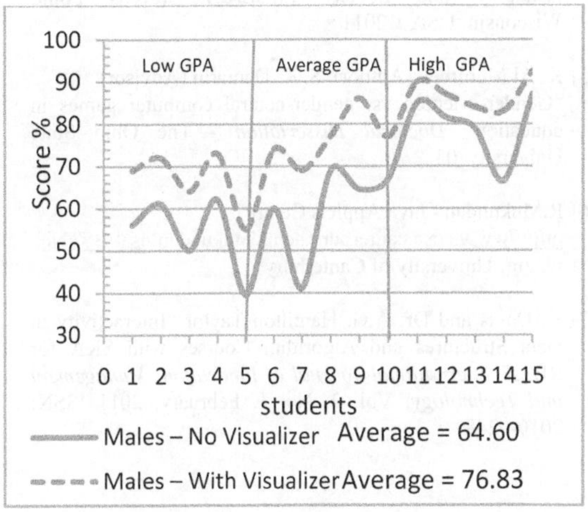

Figure 4. Male Students Test Scores

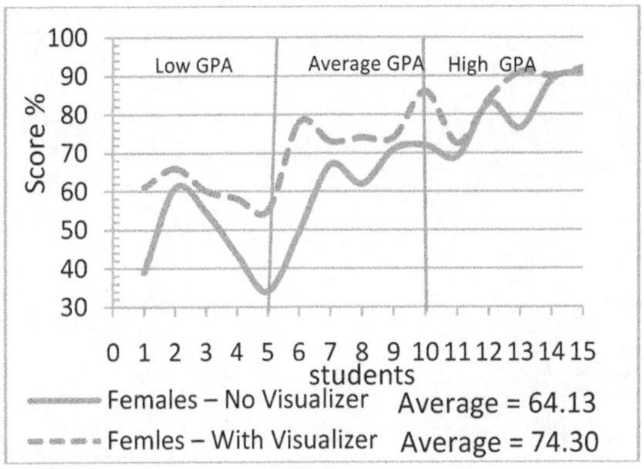

Figure 5. Female Students Test Scores

5. Conclusions, Limitations & Future Work

The effect of using the visual application tool was both as expected and somehow contrary to our expectations at the same time. Both males and females average exam grade improved as a result of using the visualizer. However, they increased from 64.6% to 76.83% for males and from 64.13% to 74.30% for females. This leads to one of two conclusions:

(a) Although we predicted that males would *like* the visual learning technique more than females, they are not necessarily increasing their understanding of the underlying complexities at a rate that is large enough to justify the initial hypothesis

or

(b) Female students are as amenable [15] to visualizer aids as male counterparts, and that they are at least as capable of transforming fun to knowledge of the concepts as their male counterparts.

It is well established in almost all references in this paper that visual aids and multimedia add significant pedagogical value in education. We set out to test this phenomenon with a specific, fairly complex computer science sub-field and have found that these subjects are just as amenable to education aids as others. We also found that, even though, we assumed that gender will constitute a significant factor in the study, it turned out to be almost negligible.

There are limitations in this work; a significant one is the sample sizes. 20 students in each group is a very good sample size for illustrating a phenomenon, however, we would like to test the effect of visual aids on learning algorithms with 200 or more students to get a better impression of the effect, this will be our next step, although controlling 200 students in terms of *sample pollution* is likely to be significantly more difficult.

The other limitation in our work, which is less serious, is that our application is written in Java, even though it aids C++ learning, which is the programming language used in class. Our visual aid does not include video and audio features, nor did we test the effects of such aids on different age groups in the college. We anticipate these areas can be touched upon in future work.

In conclusion, the visualizer presented here did have a significant and positive effect on the performance and therefore the understanding of the students of the Data Structures course. As such, it constitutes a good eLearning tool to support the traditional in-class and lab teaching methods.

6. References

[1] W. H. Ford and W. R. Topp "Data Structures with C++ using STL" Second Edition. Prentice Hall. '02

[2] J. Beidler "Data Structures and Algorithms" Springer Verlag. '97

[3] S. Shabanah, J. Chen, H. Wechsler, D. Carr and E. Wegman "Designing Computer Games to Teach Algorithms" Proc. *2010 Seventh International Conference on Information Technology, ITNG '10*

[4] Budd, Timothy, "Classic Data Structures in Java" Addison Wesley Longman. '01.

[5] A. Schalk, J. Juan Palacios-Perez "Concrete Data Structures as Games" *Electronic Notes in Theoretical Computer Science (ENTCS)* Volume 122, Elsevier Science Publishers B. V. March '05

[6] A. S. Erkan, T. J. VanSlyke and T. M. Scaffidi "Data structure visualization with latex and prefuse" Proc. *12th annual SIGCSE conference on Innovation and technology in computer science education* ITiCSE June '07

[7] M. L. Model "Data structures, data abstraction: a contemporary introduction using C++" Prentice-Hall, Inc. January '94

[8] A. Drozdek "Data Structures and Algorithms in Java" Brooks Cole. '01

[9] T. L. Naps, G. Rossling, V. Almstrum, W. Dann, R. Fleischer, C. Hundhausen, A. Korhonen, L. Malmi, M. McNally, S. Rodger, and J. A. Velazquez-Iturbide "Exploring the role of visualization and engagement in computer science education" *ITiCSE-WGR '02: Working group reports from ITiCSE on Innovation and technology in computer science education*, Aarhus. ACM Press, '02, pp. 131–152

[10] Kris M. Y. Law, Victor C. S. Lee, Y. T. Yu "Learning motivation in e-learning facilitated computer programming courses" *Computers & Education* , Volume 55 Issue 1 Elsevier Science Ltd. August '10

[11] H. Tüzün, M. Yılmaz-Soylu, T. Karakuş, Y. İnal, G. Kızılkaya "The effects of computer games on primary school students' achievement and motivation in geography learning" *Computers & Education* , Volume 52 Issue 1 Elsevier Science Ltd. January '09

[12] R. Lawrence "Teaching data structures using competitive games" *IEEE Transactions on Education* Volume 47, Issue 4 pp 459 – 466 NOV '04

[13] M. P. Chen, L. C. Wang "The Effects of Type of Interactivity in Experiential Game-Based Learning" Graduate Institute of Information and Computer Education, National Taiwan Normal University, Taipei, Taiwan 10610 Proc. *4th International Conference on E-Learning and Games: Learning by Playing. Game-based Education System Design and Development* Edutainment '09

[14] J. C. Yen, J. Y. Wang and I. J. Chen"Gender differences in mobile game-based learning to promote intrinsic motivation" Proc. *15th WSEAS international conference on Computers* World Scientific and Engineering Academy and Society (WSEAS) Stevens Point, Wisconsin, USA ©2011

[15] K. Al Mubireek (Author), S. K. Damarin (Advisor) "Gender-oriented vs. gender-neutral computer games in education" *Doctoral Dissertation* - The Ohio State University '03

[16] R.Mukundan "Java Applets Centre" http://www.cosc.canterbury.ac.nz/mukundan/dsal/BSTNew.htm, University of Canterbury

[17] K. Davis and Dr. A.G. Hamilton Taylor "Interactivity in Data Structures and Algorithm Courses with SKA for RBTs" *International Journal of Innovation, Management and Technology*, Vol. 2, No. 1, February, 2011 ISSN: 2010-0248

Generation and Rendering of Fractal Terrains on Approximated Spherical Surfaces

J. M. Willemse and K. A. Hawick
Computer Science, Institute of Natural and Mathematical Sciences
Massey University, Albany, New Zealand
email: { j.m.willemse, k.a.hawick }@massey.ac.nz
Tel: +64 9 414 0800 Fax: +64 9 441 8181

Abstract— *Terrain modelling and rendering is an important aspect of modern computer games, computer generated scene rendering in movies and is also used in scientific simulations and geographic modelling. Rendering a planetary surface without polar geometry issues has long been a difficult problem, and this is exacerbated when simulation models need approximately smooth and equal areas. We have developed a terrain approximation algorithm suited for planetary surfaces, that achieves a reasonably uniform spherical approximation by combining polyhedral subdivision and midpoint displacement. We give details of the algorithm and some examples of its use.*

Keywords: Fractal Terrain, Geodesic Mesh Generation, Midpoint Displacement, Polyhedral Subdivision

1. Introduction

Generating and rendering realistic planetary surfaces is an important problem for computer games, movies and animations. It is also useful for testing various geospatial simulation models. Although it has been known since the work of Mandelbrot and others [1] that realistic height elevation maps are fractal in nature it is not trivial to generate a reaslistic looking height model that is free of any algorithmic artifacts. Generating a suitable map on a spherical mesh that is approximately equal area and which is therefore suitable for a simulated planetary surface presents further challenges.

A new technique for generating a simulated model of terrestrial bodies is presented in this paper. The algorithm is a hybrid of an existing method to create fractal terrain known as midpoint displacement and an existing method to generate geodesic spherical approximations by polyhedral subdivision. The aim of this research has been to investigate means of generating artificial planets where the surface has realistic terrain rather than employing textures to give the illusion of terrain. Potential applications of this *Fractal Planet* algorithm are in the computer graphics field. For example, in video game maps where it is necessary to have an unbounded, but finite surface. Commonly, but rather unrealistically, this is achieved with rectangular or square maps with periodic boundary conditions, effectively forming a toroidal surface. Usually, players are oblivious to this when they view the world from a first or third person perspective. Another potential purpose, applicable to the research interests of the authors is in the field of complex systems and simulations. A fractal planet surface presents a new paradigm for lattice-based and particle simulations where elevation and proximity to water can have significance.

1.1 Related Works

A 1982 article by Alan Fournier, et. al. [2] is widely attributed with the introduction of the concept of stochastic terrain models. This work was discussed further by Gavin Miller [3]. The diamond-square algorithm [2] is still widely used in graphical applications and is a very good approximation of mountainous landscapes on flat meshes.

A method to procedurally generate planet-like meshes using a region tree is discussed in [4] and another spherical terrain renderer using the HEALPix grid [5] is presented in [6]. These techniques include consideration for dynamic level of detail on a spherical coordinate systems and are ideal for visually aesthetic computer graphics, whereas, the work presented in this particular paper focuses on the generation of the grid and the application of fractal terrain as a parametrisable aspect for triangular or by extent hexagonal lattice simulations.

Simulations which may be modified and performed on a *Fractal Planet* include, but are not limited to Lotka-Volterra predator-prey models [7], [8], epidemiology models and Gaia hypotheses models such as Daisyworld [9].

2. Fractal Terrain

Terrain can be described as a fractal phenomena in that any subset and magnification is self-similar. I.e., Statistically, all subsets have an equivalent signature to any other subset or the whole. This can be represented computationally by the midpoint displacement technique employed by the Diamond-Square algorithm [2].

Figure 1 is a two-dimensional rendering of an arbitrary terrain created using the diamond-square algorithm. With no additional data, the same values used to generate the two-dimensional image can be used to create a three-dimensional

Fig. 1: A two-dimensional height map generated with the diamond-square algorithm

Fig. 2: A three-dimensional visualisation of terrain generated with the diamond-square algorithm

representation of the terrain. Consider that figure 2 is rendered within a three-dimensional Cartesian coordinate system; for each (x, y, z) coordinate, only the y value is determined by the algorithm, x and z are regular discrete intervals. Therefore, the y data can be algorithmically determined and stored in a simple array or matrix. Both interpretations can be tiled seamlessly forming a theoretical torus.

The diamond-square algorithm begins with a matrix of uninstantiated y values except for the four corners, which are seeded with the value 0. There are two recursive steps which are repeated until all cells of the matrix have been set. The diamond step sets the midpoint of every square of set cells, effectively forming diamond shapes, the square step sets the midpoint of the vertical and horizontal lines of each diamond, forming squares once again. Figure 3 demonstrates this algorithm. The value given to each new set cell is determined by the average of the the set points surrounding the new cell, plus some random value in a delta-height range. This range is reduced at each recursive step by multiplying

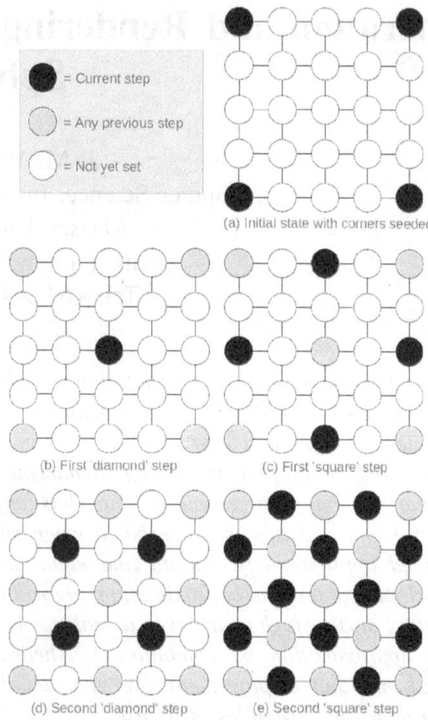

Fig. 3: Steps of the diamond-square algorithm

by a roughness constant $\in [0, 1]$, so as the resolution of the set points increases, the possible displacement range decreases.

The midpoint displacement concept is applied to the fractal displacement technique of the *Fractal Planet* algorithm presented in this work. See section 4.3.

3. Spherical Geodesic Grids

The motivation behind employing spherical geodesic grids arises from the inherent problem due to the meridian convergence on latitude-longitude grids. I.e., the constant longitudinal lines converge at the poles of the sphere causing higher vertex resolution at the poles than the equatorial line [10]. This is not considered such a problem on spherical approximations where the surface is smooth. However, as this work aims to introduce terrain-like elevation variance to the surface, it is important to have an approximately uniform vertex resolution. This can be achieved by recursive subdivision of regular convex polyhedra (platonic solids) [11].

In this work, the simplest of all of the platonic solids, a tetrahedron, is used for a reason which is explained in section 4. The tetrahedron's four equilateral triangle sides are created with four vertices, each with a magnitude of one unit, i.e., a normalised vector (See table 2). This tetrahedron can be thought to be a sphere approximation of the lowest

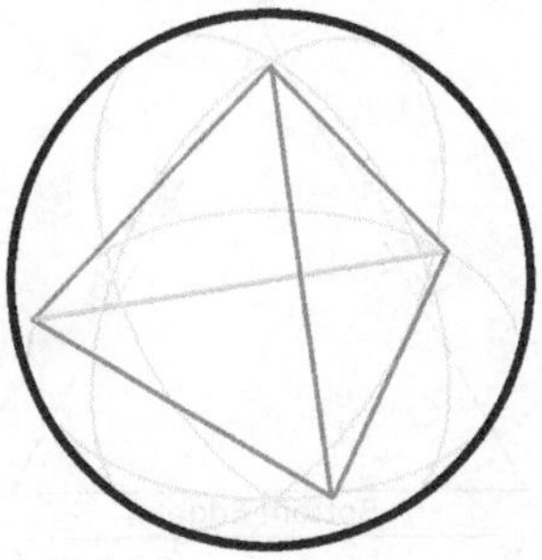

Fig. 4: A normalised regular tetrahedron bounded by a unit sphere

possible resolution. Figure 4 illustrates a tetrahedron with a bounding unit sphere. All four vertices are located at a point on the surface of the unit sphere.

Upon subdividing the initial tetrahedron, a new vertex is added at the middle point of each edge. Each edge belongs to two faces. Connecting the three new vertices belonging to each face results in one triangle becoming four. Of course, simply adding new vertices does not create a better spherical approximation. All new vertices must also be extended to the unit sphere such that their magnitude is equivalent to the original vertices. This is achieved by vector normalisation (Equation 1).

$$\hat{v} = \frac{v}{\|v\|} = \left(\frac{x}{\|v\|}, \frac{y}{\|v\|}, \frac{z}{\|v\|}\right) \tag{1}$$

Obviously, the further the tetrahedron is subdivided, the higher the resolution of the approximated sphere. There is no need to keep track of each vertex in memory. Although multiple faces share a given vertex, the calculation to determine the new vertex's position is simple enough that it can be processed on a face-by-face basis. Effectively calculating the position of the same vertex twice. However, once fractal terrain is introduced, the vertex positions are non-deterministic and therefore, must be calculated only once and referenced by each face that uses it, so as to prevent disconnected edges between faces. This is the main problem addressed by the *Fractal Planet* algorithm.

4. Fractal Planet Algorithm

The *Fractal Planet* algorithm combines spherical approximation by polyhedral subdivision and midpoint displacement techniques to achieve a sphere based rendering model with seamless fractal landscapes without bump or texture mapping. The stochastic nature of this algorithm means that, while certain attributes can be specified and the general appearance of the planet will always be statistically fractal (i.e., self-similar), continent size, location and elevation are non-deterministic.

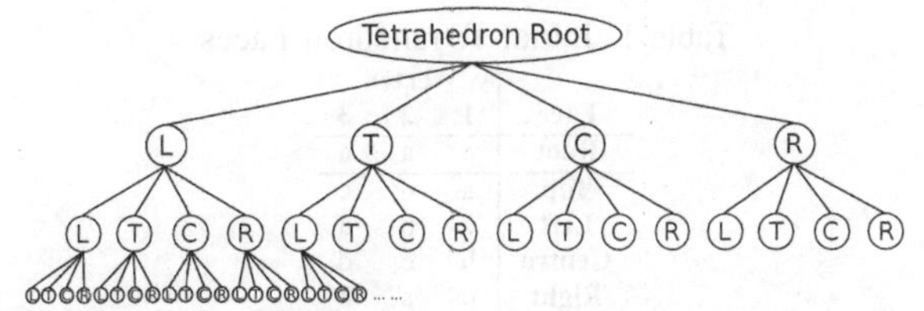

Fig. 5: Tree structure demonstrating the node associativity of the subdivided tetrahedron

In essence, the *Fractal Planet* algorithm is a particular quad-tree traversal technique used to find vertex associativity on a spherical approximation formed by the recursive subdivision of a tetrahedron. The technique relies on the triangular geometry of the faces forming the sphere.

4.1 Quad-Tree Data Structure

A spherical approximation generated by tetrahedron subdivision is usually rendered by vertices which are exclusive to a single face. Such that, although there are commonly six triangular faces (five at the net corners) which share a vertex in theory, each vertex of a face is simply determined by assuming the normalised midpoint of all edges of the previous level of subdivision. With the introduction of fractal terrain to a spherical surface, this property is no longer valid.

A quad-tree is an obvious solution for storing references to triangular faces. Consider that each node of the quad-tree is a triangle containing three vertices which define it in three-dimensional space and three initially unused mid-point vertices which, once subdivided, will reference the new vertices along each of a triangles three edges. All six of the mentioned vertices will be referenced by a pointer to the memory location at which each is stored. These pointers will be reused by six triangles for the most part, but by five triangles at the four vertices of the initial polyhedron. Figure 5 shows the basic quad-tree structure.

The polyhedron used within this work is a regular tetrahedron for the simple reason that its net is a triangle itself. This inherent property lends itself well to the quad-tree of triangle nodes in that the root node of the tree is the net. It is a slightly special case, however, as its three defining vertex pointers are all references to the same memory location – vertex a (see table 1 and figure 6). The nature of the tetrahedron also means the three mid-point edge vertices are given – vertices b, c and d. The four given tetrahedron vertices must be at positions on the unit sphere. Table 2 shows these initial normalised vector values.

To determine the path to a neighbour of any given node in the mesh, the "Three Adjacency" rules can be applied to the path of the known node. The rules are basic and rely on two things. Firstly, all nodes must know their own quad-tree path including their child type (e.g., Left, Top, Centre or Right). Secondly, the three edges of every triangle are relative to their orientation (i.e., a triangle either points up or down).

Table 1: Initial Tetrahedron Faces

Face	Vertex 1	2	3
Root	a	a	a
Top	a	d	c
Left	c	b	a
Centre	b	c	d
Right	d	a	b

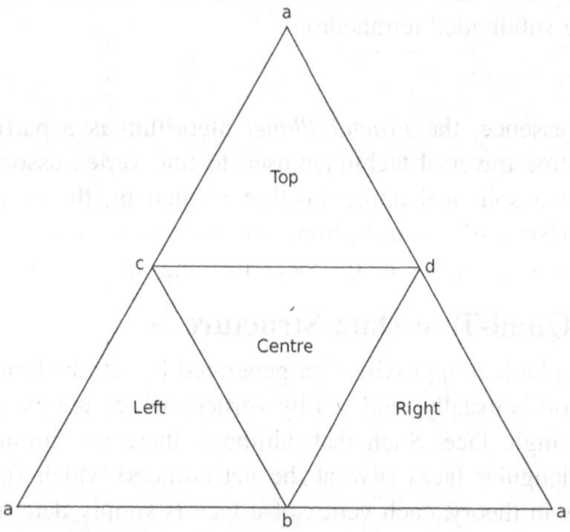

Fig. 6: The net of a regular tetrahedron

If a triangle is pointed upward relative to the perspective of the viewer, the left, right and bottom edges are exactly as labelled. However, a downward pointing triangle's left edge and right edges are opposite to the viewer's perspective and the bottom edge is the horizontal edge on top. See figure 7.

Table 3 illustrates the aforementioned rules. In order to apply the rules, take the path of the current node and determine the most recent common ancestor node of it and its desired neighbour node by traversing its path in reverse order until a 'C' (Centre) or the "opposite" node type is reached (i.e., L and R, and T and C are opposites). Apply the swap rules for the appropriate edge to each node in the path after and including the determined most recent common ancestor. For example, in figure 8 take the node with the path "CCLLL", based on the above, the most recent common ancestor of it and its left neighbour is the second 'C', therefore, from this node onward, we apply the "Left Edge Rule", resulting in "C, C→R, L→T, L→T, L→T" ("CCTTT"). Also note that the left neighbour of "CCTTT" is the original example node "CCLLL", which means all left

Table 2: Initial Tetrahedron Vertices [11]

Vertex	x	y	z
a	0.0	0.0	1.0
b	0.0	0.942809	-0.333333
c	0.816497	-0.471405	-0.333333
d	-0.816497	-0.471405	-0.333333

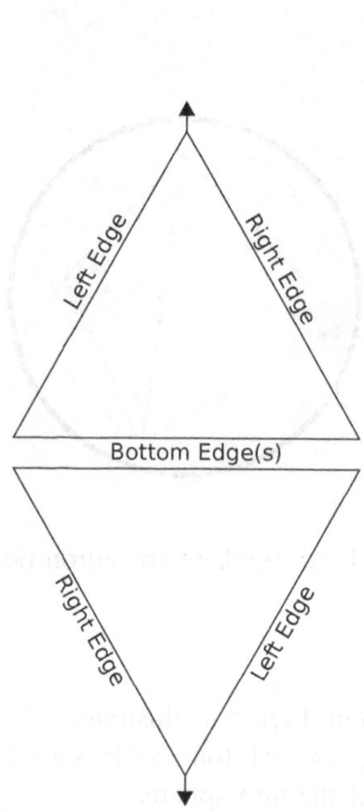

Fig. 7: Triangular nodes with edge labels relative to the orientation of the triangle

Table 3: Rules for Determining the Quad-Tree Paths of the *Three-Adjacency* Neighbours of a Triangle Node

Bottom Edge	Left Edge	Right Edge
$T \leftrightarrow C$	$C \leftrightarrow R$	$L \leftrightarrow C$
$L \leftrightarrow R$	$L \leftrightarrow T$	$T \leftrightarrow R$

neighbours of node x have x as their left neighbour too. The same applies for all edges and nodes.

Algorithm 1 explains the key data structure used for the quad-tree. Before new nodes can be added to the tree, they must be created through a subdivision technique, as discussed in the following subsection.

4.2 Iterative Subdivision

After the initial tetrahedron is defined, the subdivision of the faces takes place. A level of subdivision (N) must be given as a number of times the tree will be divided. A breadth-first traversal of the tree occurs inside a loop (algorithm 2) and each leaf node is subdivided into four new child nodes where the vertex associativity between neighbour nodes occurs in order to determine whether a desired vertex already exists. Algorithm 3 explains this in detail.

4.3 Fractal Displacement

Algorithm 4 shows how displacements are calculated using a delta height range and the average unit vector offset of the two vertices of which the new node is the dividing midpoint.

Where (a, b, c) occur in Algorithms 1 to 4, the points in respective order are clockwise from the relative *top* of their triangle. Figure 6 illustrates the original vertices and the make up of the four faces of the tetrahedron. Figure 7

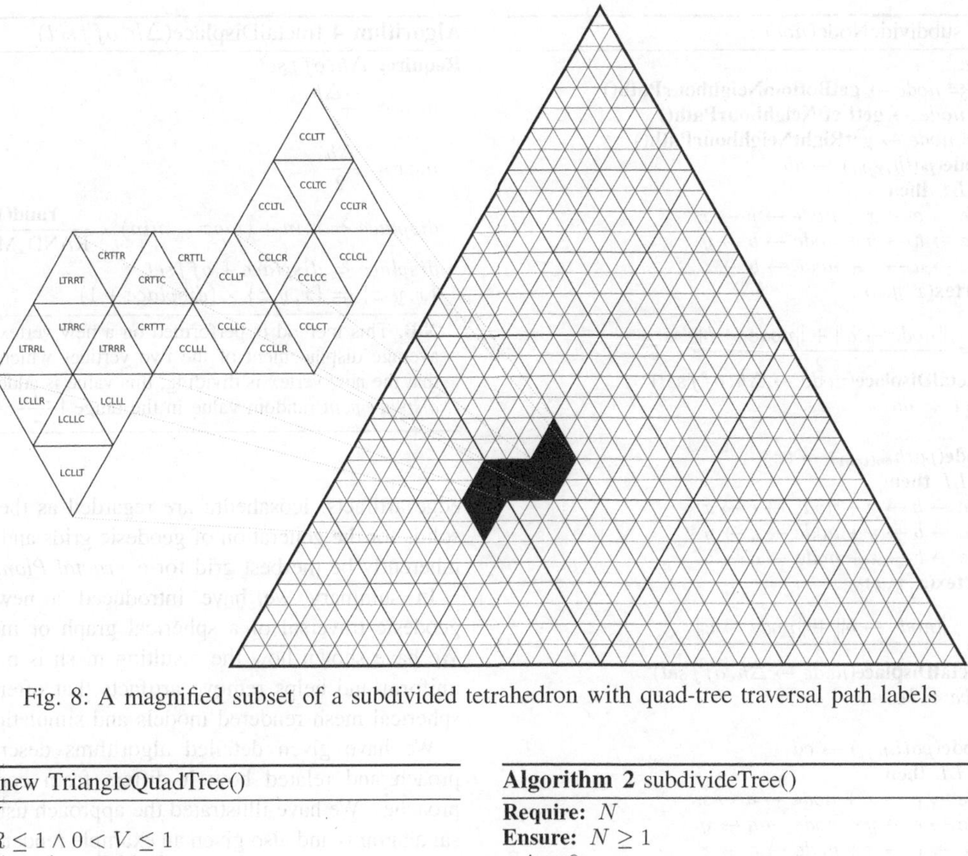

Fig. 8: A magnified subset of a subdivided tetrahedron with quad-tree traversal path labels

---

Algorithm 1 new TriangleQuadTree()

Require: R, V
Ensure: $0 < R \leq 1 \wedge 0 < V \leq 1$
  $tetra \rightarrow (a, b, c, d) \Leftarrow$ **Table 2**
  $root \rightarrow (a, b, c) \Leftarrow tetra \rightarrow (a, a, a)$
  $root \rightarrow \Delta h \Leftarrow V$
  $root \rightarrow parent \Leftarrow NULL$
  $root \rightarrow ab \Leftarrow tetra \rightarrow d$
  $root \rightarrow bc \Leftarrow tetra \rightarrow b$
  $root \rightarrow ca \Leftarrow tetra \rightarrow c$
  $root \rightarrow L \rightarrow (a, b, c) \Leftarrow tetra \rightarrow (c, b, a)$
  $root \rightarrow T \rightarrow (a, b, c) \Leftarrow tetra \rightarrow (a, d, c)$
  $root \rightarrow C \rightarrow (a, b, c) \Leftarrow tetra \rightarrow (b, c, d)$
  $root \rightarrow R \rightarrow (a, b, c) \Leftarrow tetra \rightarrow (d, a, b)$
  $root \rightarrow \{L, T, C, R\} \rightarrow parent \Leftarrow root$
  $root \rightarrow \{L, T, C, R\} \rightarrow \Delta h \Leftarrow root \rightarrow \Delta h \times R$
  $this \rightarrow$ **subdivideTree**() [Algorithm 2]

N.B. a, b, c, d, ab, bc and ca are three-dimensional vertices. $root$, $parent$, L (left), T (top), C (centre) and R (right) are triangle tree nodes which contain three major vertices (a, b, c) and three subdivision vertices (ab, bc, ca) which are $NULL$ unless otherwise assigned (i.e., $NULL$ for leaf nodes), each node also contains five pointers to other nodes $(parent, L, T, C, R)$. $tetra$ is the collective term for the hard-coded initial vertices which form a regular unit-tetrahedron, Δh is the range of a triangles node's potential elevation displacement ($[\frac{-\Delta h}{2}, \frac{\Delta h}{2}]$), this value is determined by the elevation variance constant V for the $root$, each subdivided node's Δh is its parents Δh value multiplied by the roughness constant R.

---

demonstrates the relative left, right and top points of a triangle based on its directional orientation.

Algorithm 2 subdivideTree()

Require: N
Ensure: $N \geq 1$
  $i \Leftarrow 0$
  while $i < N$ **do**
    $q \Leftarrow$ **Queue**()
    $q \rightarrow push(root \rightarrow \{L, T, C, R\})$
    $t \Leftarrow NULL$
    while $q \rightarrow size() \neq 0$ **do**
      $t \Leftarrow q \rightarrow front()$
      $q \rightarrow pop()$
      if $t \rightarrow \{L, T, C, R\} \neq NULL$ **then**
        $q \rightarrow push(t \rightarrow \{L, T, C, R\})$
      else
        subdivideNode(t) [Algorithm 3]
      end if
    end while
    $i \Leftarrow i + 1$
  end while

N.B. This method iterates over the tree N times, each time creating a new level of subdivision. q is a queue data structure used to traverse the current state of the quad-tree in breadth-first order. The $root$ triangle node's children (L, T, C and R) are pushed to the queue. t is assigned the front value of q in a loop and t's children are added to q if they exist. However, if t does not have any children, a leaf node has been reached and that node is subdivided.

---

5. Future Work and Conclusions

The tetrahedron was selected for this work for its simplicity. It is the most basic of the platonic solids in terms of the

Algorithm 3 subdivideNode($node$)

Require: $node$
$path_{bottom} \Leftarrow node \rightarrow$ **getBottomNeighbourPath()**
$path_{left} \Leftarrow node \rightarrow$ **getLeftNeighbourPath()**
$path_{right} \Leftarrow node \rightarrow$ **getRightNeighbourPath()**
$ab \Leftarrow$ **getNode**($path_{right}$) $\rightarrow ab$
if $ab \equiv NULL$ **then**
$x \Leftarrow node \rightarrow a \rightarrow x + node \rightarrow b \rightarrow x$
$y \Leftarrow node \rightarrow a \rightarrow y + node \rightarrow b \rightarrow y$
$z \Leftarrow node \rightarrow a \rightarrow z + node \rightarrow b \rightarrow z$
$ab \Leftarrow$ **Vertex**(x, y, z)
$ab \Leftarrow \widehat{ab}$
$offset \Leftarrow \frac{\|node \rightarrow a\| + \|node \rightarrow b\|}{2} - 1$
$ab \rightarrow$ **fractalDisplace**($node \rightarrow \Delta h, offset$)
$node \rightarrow ab \Leftarrow ab$
end if
$bc \Leftarrow$ **getNode**($path_{bottom}$) $\rightarrow bc$
if $bc \equiv NULL$ **then**
$x \Leftarrow node \rightarrow b \rightarrow x + node \rightarrow c \rightarrow x$
$y \Leftarrow node \rightarrow b \rightarrow y + node \rightarrow c \rightarrow y$
$z \Leftarrow node \rightarrow b \rightarrow z + node \rightarrow c \rightarrow z$
$bc \Leftarrow$ **Vertex**(x, y, z)
$bc \Leftarrow \widehat{bc}$
$offset \Leftarrow \frac{\|node \rightarrow b\| + \|node \rightarrow c\|}{2} - 1$
$bc \rightarrow$ **fractalDisplace**($node \rightarrow \Delta h, offset$)
$node \rightarrow bc \Leftarrow bc$
end if
$ca \Leftarrow$ **getNode**($path_{left}$) $\rightarrow ca$
if $ca \equiv NULL$ **then**
$x \Leftarrow node \rightarrow c \rightarrow x + node \rightarrow a \rightarrow x$
$y \Leftarrow node \rightarrow c \rightarrow y + node \rightarrow a \rightarrow y$
$z \Leftarrow node \rightarrow c \rightarrow z + node \rightarrow a \rightarrow z$
$ca \Leftarrow$ **Vertex**(x, y, z)
$ca \Leftarrow \widehat{ca}$
$offset \Leftarrow \frac{\|node \rightarrow c\| + \|node \rightarrow a\|}{2} - 1$
$ca \rightarrow$ **fractalDisplace**($node \rightarrow \Delta h, offset$)
$node \rightarrow ca \Leftarrow ca$
end if
$node \rightarrow L \Leftarrow$ **Node**($node, LEFT, ca, bc, node \rightarrow c$)
$node \rightarrow T \Leftarrow$ **Node**($node, TOP, node \rightarrow a, ab, ca$)
$node \rightarrow C \Leftarrow$ **Node**($node, CENTRE, bc, ca, ab$)
$node \rightarrow R \Leftarrow$ **Node**($node, RIGHT, ab, node \rightarrow b, bc$)

N.B. The three **get*NeighbourPath()** methods apply the three-adjacency rules to the path of a node in order to determine the neighbour paths (See table 3). **getNode**($path$) returns a triangle node by traversing the route given by the path argument. **fractalDisplace**($\Delta h, offset$) is described in Algorithm 4. The **Node**($node, TYPE, a, b, c$) constructor creates a new triangle node where $node$ is the parent, $TYPE$ is the child type and a, b and c are the vertices which make up the triangle (clockwise from relative top).

number of faces and vertices required to construct it. The equilateral triangle shape of its net is the same as the shape of its faces and therefore, accommodated for a simple quad-tree structure of triangular nodes where the root node is the tetrahedron itself. In future works, the use of other, more complicated platonic solids will be explored. The presumed advantage of this is the reduction in the severity of the fold-

Algorithm 4 fractalDisplace($\Delta h, offset$)

Require: $\Delta h, offset$
$min \Leftarrow \frac{-\Delta h}{2}$
$max \Leftarrow \frac{\Delta h}{2}$
$displace \Leftarrow min + (max - min) \times \frac{\textbf{rand()}}{\text{RAND\_MAX}}$
$displace \Leftarrow displace + offset$
$\{x, y, z\} \Leftarrow \{x, y, z\} \times (displace + 1)$

N.B. This method is performed on a new vertex, $offset$ is the average displacement of the two vertices which form the edge that the new vertex is dividing, this value is added to a *midpoint displacement* random value in the range $[\frac{-\Delta h}{2}, \frac{\Delta h}{2}]$

edge artifacts. Icosahedra are regarded as the best platonic solids for the generation of geodesic grids and will therefore inherently be the best grid for a *Fractal Planet*.

In summary we have introduced a new method for geodesic traversal of a spherical graph or mesh of points. We have shown how the resulting mesh is both reasonably uniform and helps remove artifacts that often spoil typical spherical mesh rendered models and simulations.

We have given detailed algorithms describing the approach and related how it differs from conventional approaches. We have illustrated the approach using tree traversal diagrams and also given an example rendering of a fractal landscape generated on our spherical mesh.

We believe our algorithm and approach has scope for rendering a number of planetary surface area based simulation models that are based on localised interactions and which need a systematic neighbour determination algorithm.

Figure 9 shows a sample rendering of a planetary elevation map surface generated by the algorithm.

References

[1] Benoit B. Mandelbrot. *The Fractal Geometry of Nature*. W.H. Freeman, 1982.

[2] Alain Fournier, Don Fussell, and Loren Carpenter. Computer rendering of stochastic models. *Commun. ACM*, 25(6):371–384, Jun 1982.

[3] Gavin S P Miller. The definition and rendering of terrain maps. In *Proceedings of the 13th annual conference on Computer graphics and interactive techniques*, SIGGRAPH '86, pages 39–48, New York, NY, USA, 1986. ACM.

[4] Felix Haase, Maximilian Klein, Andreas Tarnowsky, and Franz-Erich Wolter. Interactive fractal compositions. In *Proceedings of the 11th ACM SIGGRAPH International Conference on Virtual-Reality Continuum and its Applications in Industry*, VRCAI '12, pages 181–188, New York, NY, USA, 2012. ACM.

[5] K. M. Górski, E. Hivon, A. J. Banday, B. D. Wandelt, F. K. Hansen, M. Reinecke, and M. Bartelmann. HEALPix: A Framework for High-Resolution Discretization and Fast Analysis of Data Distributed on the Sphere. *Am. J. Phys.*, 622:759–771, apr 2005.

[6] Rolf Westerteiger, Andreas Gerndt, and Bernd Hamann. Spherical Terrain Rendering using the hierarchical HEALPix grid. In Christoph Garth, Ariane Middel, and Hans Hagen, editors, *Visualization of Large and Unstructured Data Sets: Applications in Geospatial Planning, Modeling and Engineering - Proceedings of IRTG 1131 Workshop 2011*, volume 27 of *OpenAccess Series in Informatics (OASIcs)*, pages

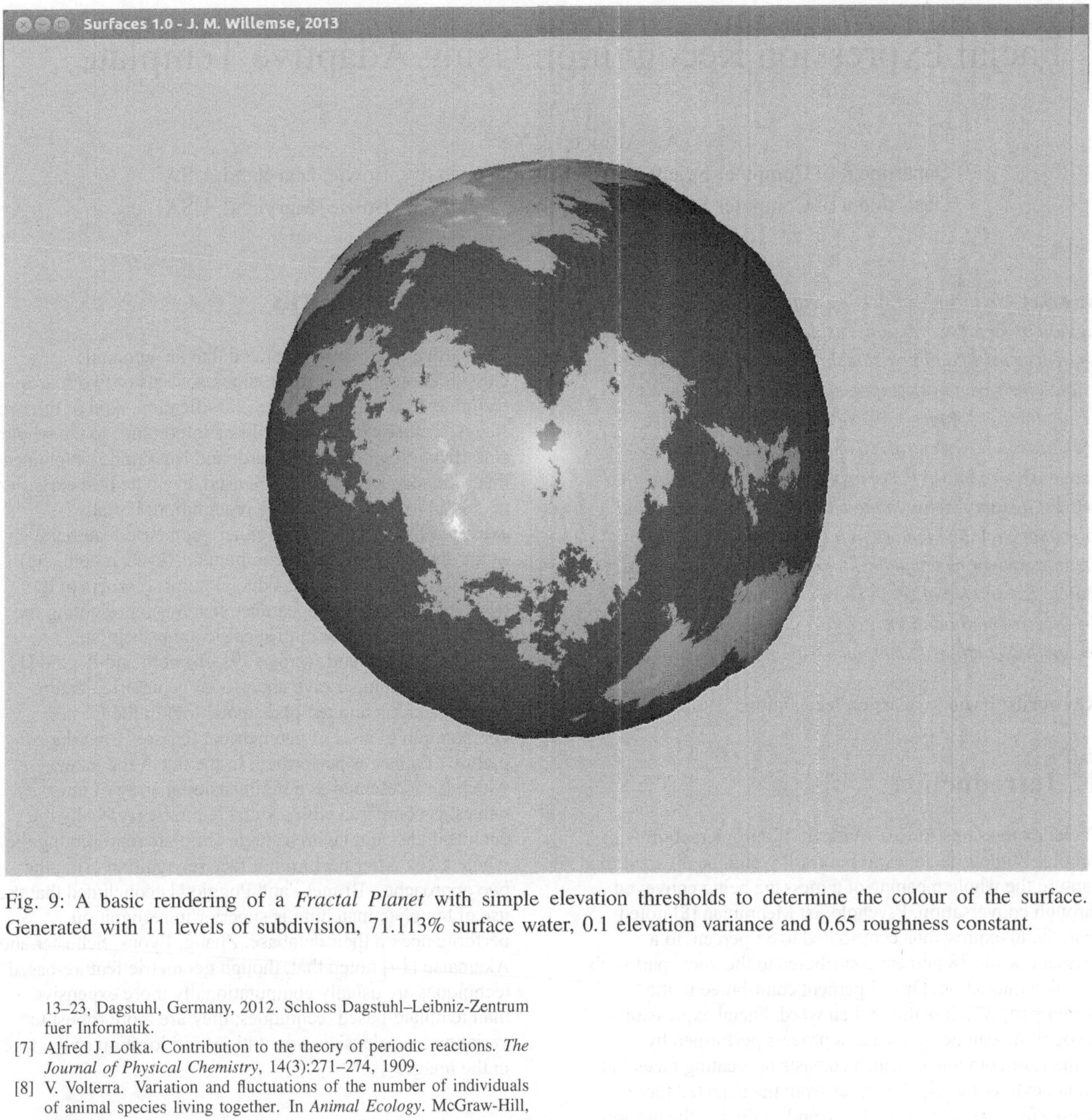

Fig. 9: A basic rendering of a *Fractal Planet* with simple elevation thresholds to determine the colour of the surface. Generated with 11 levels of subdivision, 71.113% surface water, 0.1 elevation variance and 0.65 roughness constant.

13–23, Dagstuhl, Germany, 2012. Schloss Dagstuhl–Leibniz-Zentrum fuer Informatik.

[7] Alfred J. Lotka. Contribution to the theory of periodic reactions. *The Journal of Physical Chemistry*, 14(3):271–274, 1909.

[8] V. Volterra. Variation and fluctuations of the number of individuals of animal species living together. In *Animal Ecology*. McGraw-Hill, 1926.

[9] Andrew J. Watson and James E. Lovelock. Biological homeostasis of the global environment: the parable of daisyworld. *Tellus B*, 35B(4):284–289, 1983.

[10] D.A. Randall, T.D. Ringler, R.P. Heikes, P. Jones, and J. Baumgardner. Climate modeling with spherical geodesic grids. *Computing in Science Engineering*, 4(5):32–41, Sep/Oct 2002.

[11] Edward Angel and Dave Shreiner. *Interactive Computer Graphics: A Top Down Approach with Shader-Based OpenGL*. Addison-Wesley, Boston, 6 edition, 2012.

Facial Expression Recognition Using Adaptive Template

A. Attipoe[1], J. Yan[2]
[1]Department of Computer Science, Bowie State University, Bowie, Maryland, USA
[2]Department of Computer Science, Bowie State University, Bowie, Maryland, USA

Abstract - *In this paper, we presented a classification method of facial expressions displayed in images or video sequences using adaptive template. In our approach, we trained the seven basic expressions templates known as "Happiness", "Anger", "Disgust", "Fear", "Surprise", "Sadness" and "Neutral". Then we take an input face image with unknown facial expressions and calculate the nearest distance between the feature points on that input face image and the feature points on each of the seven facial expressions templates, therefore to find the closest match. Experimental result shows that adaptive template is an effective method to identify facial expressions in an image that contains human face with unknown emotions.*

Keywords: Facial expression recognition, feature points

1 Introduction

Facial expressions form a vital part of our interaction with people. Without facial expressions, if would be difficult to capture the whole meaning of a message being conveyed through conversation. Psychologist Mehrabian [8] noted that, facial expressions contributed to 55 percent to a message while 38 percent contributed to the vocal part such as voice intonation. Only 7 percent contributed to the verbal part, which is the spoken word. Facial expression recognition can be defined as a process performed by humans or computers, which consists of locating faces in a scene, extracting facial features from the detected face region(facial feature extraction), and analyzing the motion of the facial feature and/or the changes in the appearance of the facial features and classifying this information into some facial expression–interpretative categories such as facial muscle activations like smile, emotion categories like anger or attitude categories like (dis)liking [9]. Adaptive templates help us capture facial expressions variations or deformations. In our approach, we classify facial expression using adaptive templates.

2 Related Works

Lajevardi and Hussain [5] stated that an automatic classification of facial expressions consists of two stages: feature extraction and feature classification. And of the two stages, feature extraction is of key importance to the whole classification process. Lajevardi and Hussain [5] explained that, if inadequate features are used, even the best classifier could fail to achieve accurate recognition. Usually, extracted facial features are either geometric features such as the shapes of the facial components (eyes, mouth, etc) and the locations of facial fiducial points (corners of the eyes, mouth, etc), or appearance features representing the texture of the facial skin in specific areas including wrinkles, bulges, and furrows [9]. Brunelli and Poggio [1] performed a comparative analysis of geometric, feature-based matching and template matching. In the former, computation of a set of geometrical features from the picture of a face is performed. In the latter, the image, which is represented as a bidimensional array of intensity values, is compared with a suitable metric (typically the euclidean distance) with a single template representing the whole face. After performing face recognition using the two approaches, Brunelli and Poggio [1] concluded that the use of template matching is superior in recognition performance on their database. Zhang, Lyons, Schuster and Akamatsu [14] noted that, though geometric feature-based techniques are usually computationally more expensive than template-based techniques, they are more robust to variation in scale, size, orientation, and location of the face in the image.

3 Methodology

Our technique for facial expression recognition involves extracting facial features geometrically from the face region of an image and recognizing the face by classifying the extracted facial features. The processes covered in our experiment apply to images in both the training and testing set.

3.1 Data Acquisition

The images used for training and testing were taken from the Japanese Female Facial Expression database (JAFFE) and the Taiwanese Facial Expression Image Database (TFEID). The Taiwanese Facial Expression Image database consists of 7200 stimuli captured from 40 models (20 males) and (20 females), each with eight facial expressions: neutral, anger, contempt, disgust, fear, happiness, sadness and surprise. Models were asked to gaze at two different angles (0° and 45°). Each expression included two kinds of intensities (high and slight), and was captured by two CCD-cameras simultaneously with different viewing angles (0° and 45°). A combination of grayscale and color images was used. The images taken from the Japanese Female Facial Expression database consists of 219 image variations of the six basic facial expressions and the neutral facial expressions of ten Japanese female models.

We took 175 images of the different facial expressions in total from the Taiwanese Facial Expression Image Database. 140 images were used for the testing set; each of the seven facial expressions had 20 input/test images. Then 35 images were used for the training set. Each of the seven facial expressions had five, sample images. We ensured that the facial expressions chosen for the training set were posed by the same male and female models. 77 images were chosen from the Japanese Female Facial Expression database. 70 images for the testing set (ten images for each facial expression) and seven images for the training set, each image representing one of the seven facial expressions. All the images had a frontal view.

3.2 Image Pre-possessing

During image pre-processing, we scaled the images to 256x256 pixels and ensured that they were all of the same size and shape. We also normalized all the images to ensure that they had uniform intensity values.

Figure1: Above is the normalized training set for the Japanese Female Facial Expression (JAFFE) database

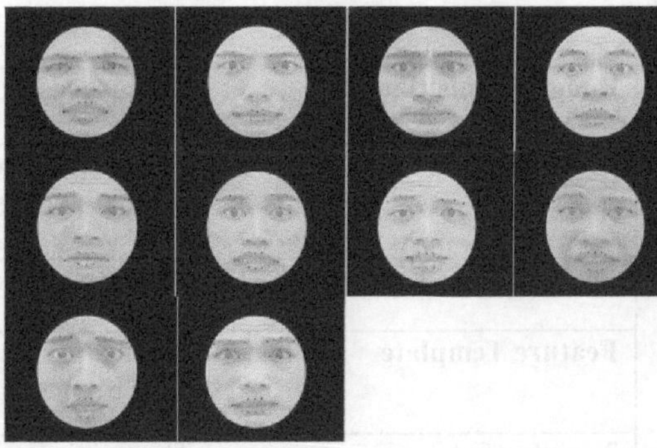

Figure 2: These *are ten* images of the "fear" facial expression in the testing set, which were taken from the Taiwanese Facial Expression Image Database and used for experimental analysis. Each of the images is 256x256 pixels.

3.3 Feature Extraction

Feature points were chosen on the face region for all the images in our training and testing set. Feature points were chosen on the eye brows, eyes and mouth on the face region of each image retrieved from the Taiwanese facial expression database. And for the images retrieved from the Japanese female facial expression database, feature points were chosen on the eye brows, eyes, mouth, chin and around the contour of the face. The goal was to use areas of the face that showed the most deformation after a facial expression has been made. For example, a surprise facial expression will show that the eye brows raised up and eyes wide open whereas a neutral facial expression will show the reverse. Each feature point on the face of an image is represented by an x-axis and a y-axis. To extract some geometric measurements from the feature points, we matched each image in our testing set against the seven facial expressions in our training set. Then we calculated the distance between the feature points located at the same location on the two images. The distance for all the feature points was calculated and summed. For each input image from our testing set, seven different distances were generated.

Image Acquisition	An image is extracted from a video sequence
Normalization	The image is normalized; it is scaled to the shape and size of the images in the training set
Feature Point Extraction	Feature points are extracted from the image
Feature Template	The feature template represents the final template after the feature points have been extracted.
Training Set	The training set contains normalized images of the seven facial expressions
Classification	The input image is classified by matching the feature template against the seven facial expressions in the training set

Table 1: These steps show the facial expression recognition approach used in our research

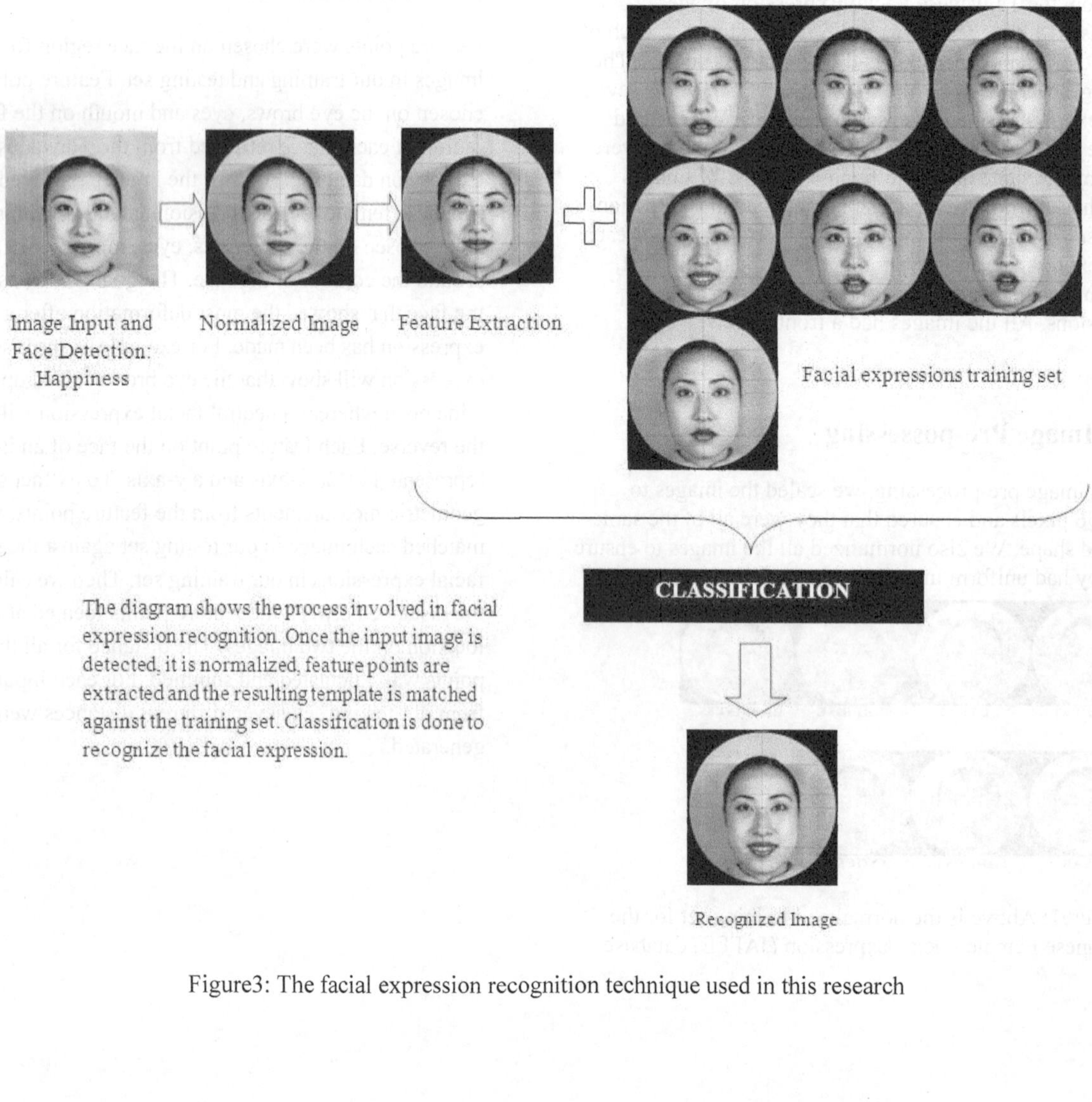

Figure3: The facial expression recognition technique used in this research

Experimental Results for <u>Disgust</u> Facial Expression
Grayscale Images – Male Models

Input Image	Anger	Disgust	Fear	Happiness	Neutral	Sadness	Surprise	Results
Image1	588.274	282.826	736.591	641.45	570.307	610.487	953.741	Matches
Image2	671.77	391.888	840.107	702.337	643.916	715.799	1029.16	Matches
Image3	707.52	373.836	832.939	679.12	662.373	689.664	1033.89	Matches
Image4	565.241	279.052	685.508	551.4	516.064	536.249	896.51	Matches
Image5	626.419	438.834	605.351	424.115	536.194	447.965	810.888	False Alarm
Image6	485.41	300.429	625.11	449.845	442.746	533.819	841.982	Matches
Image7	458.051	293.513	563.366	391.773	399.355	486.053	779.307	Matches
Image8	787.42	439.974	923.111	845.738	755.025	712.19	1060.76	Matches
Image9	601.599	328.846	734.675	613.035	548.826	585.717	925.44	Matches
Image10	467.804	349.293	632.663	632.302	434.449	607.6	867.875	Matches

Table 2: Sample results of the calculated distance for all the seven facial expressions in the training set using ten disgust input images.

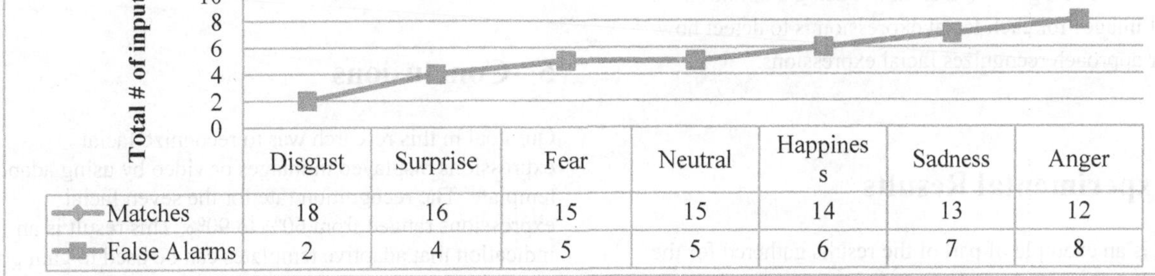

	Disgust	Surprise	Fear	Neutral	Happines s	Sadness	Anger
Matches	18	16	15	15	14	13	12
False Alarms	2	4	5	5	6	7	8

Figure 4: Each facial expression has 20 input images. The chart shows the number of input images that match the facial expressions and the number that gave false alarms.

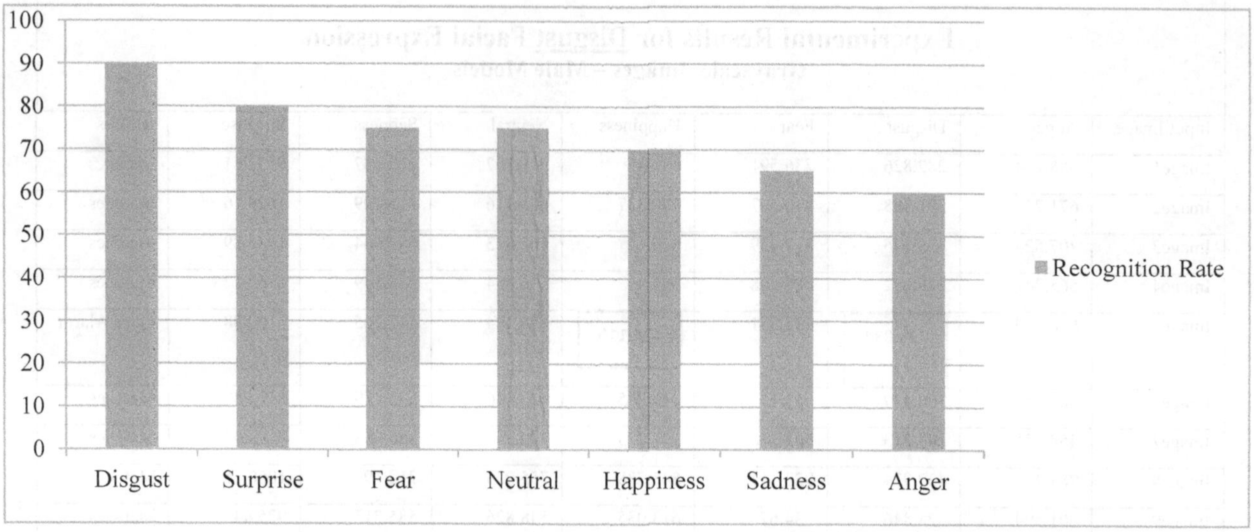

Figure 5: Shows the recognition rate for each facial expression facial expressions and the number that gave false alarms

3.4 Classification

Assuming the input image under consideration was the disgust facial expression. Matching the anger facial expression against each facial expression template will yield seven distance values. We scan through the seven distance values and choose the smallest value or shortest distance and its corresponding facial expression. Since the input image under consideration is the disgust input image, our goal is to have the shortest distance correspond to the disgust facial expression template, signifying a match and hence positive recognition. Our aim in using a minimum of 20 input images for each facial expression is to detect how well our approach recognizes facial expressions.

4 Experimental Results

Table 2 is an example of part of the results gathered for the disgust facial expression. You will notice that, for each disgust input image, the disgust image in the training set (i.e. the disgust template) had the smallest distances, except for input image5. Ten of the fear images in the testing set yielded 100% matches in the first experiment. In the second experiment, the next ten "fear" input images yielded five false alarms. The results indicated that the distance of another facial expression in the training set was smaller than the fear facial expression. In that case, our technique could not recognize the input image, which was fear. Figure 4 shows the number of matches' verses false alarms. The "disgust" facial expression had the fewest false alarms, followed by the "surprise" facial expression. The anger facial expression had the highest number of false alarms. The recognition rate for the seven facial expressions is shown in Figure 5.

5 Conclusions

Our goal in this research was to recognize facial expressions displayed in images or video by using adaptive template. The recognition rate for the seven facial expressions ranged from 60% to 90%. This result is an indication that adaptive templates can be used to gain good recognition results.

6 References

[1] R. Brunelli and T. Poggio, "Face recognition: features versus templates," *IEEE Transactions on Pattern Analysis and Machine Intelligence*, vol. 15, no. 10. pp. 1042–1052, 1993.

[2] C. Chibelushi and F. Bourel, "Facial expression recognition: A brief tutorial overview," ... : *On-Line Compendium of Computer Vision*, 2003.

[3] I. Cohen, N. Sebe, a. Garg, M. S. Lew, and T. S. Huang, "Facial expression recognition from video sequences," *Proceedings. IEEE International Conference on Multimedia and Expo*, vol. 2. Ieee, pp. 121–124.

[4] I. Cohen, N. Sebe, A. Garg, L. S. Chen, and T. S. Huang, "Facial expression recognition from video sequences: temporal and static modeling," *Computer Vision and Image Understanding*, vol. 91, no. 1–2. pp. 160–187, Jul-2003.

[5] S. Lajevardi and Z. Hussain, "Local feature extraction methods for facial expression recognition," *Proceedings of 17th European Signal* ..., 2009.

[6] P. Li, "Adaptive feature extraction and selection for robust facial expression recognition," 2010.

[7] J. J. Lien, T. Kanade, and J. F. Cohn, "Automated facial expression recognition based on FACS action units," *Proceedings Third IEEE International Conference on Automatic Face and Gesture Recognition*. IEEE Comput. Soc, pp. 390–395.

[8] A. Mehrabian, "Communication Without Words," *Psychology Today*, vol. 2, no. 9, pp. 52 – 55, 1968.

[9] M. Pantic, "Facial expression recognition," *Encyclopedia of Biometrics*. 2009.

[10] A. Ryan, J. F. Cohn, S. Lucey, J. Saragih, P. Lucey, F. De la Torre, and A. Rossi, "Automated Facial Expression Recognition System," *43rd Annual 2009 International Carnahan Conference on Security Technology*. Ieee, pp. 172–177, Oct-2009.

[11] K. Song and Y. Chen, "A design for integrated face and facial expression recognition," *IECON 2011-37th Annual Conference on* ..., 2011.

[12] F. Tang and B. Deng, "Facial Expression Recognition using AAM and Local Facial Features," *Third International Conference on Natural Computation (ICNC 2007)*. Ieee, pp. 632–635, 2007.

[13] M. Yeasin, B. Bullot, and R. Sharma, "Recognition of facial expressions and measurement of levels of interest from video," *Multimedia, IEEE Transactions* ..., 2006.

[14] Z. Zhang, M. Lyons, M. Schuster, and S. Akamatsu, "Comparison Between Geometry-Based and Gabor-Wavelets-Based Facial Expression Recognition Using Multi-Layer Perceptron," pp. 454–459, 2004.

[15] B. Zhou, X; Huang, X; Xu, "Real-Time Facial Expression Recognition Based on Boosted Embedded Hidden Markov Model," *Third International Conference on Image and Graphics (ICIG'04)*. Ieee, pp. 290–293.

Camera Tracking for Implementation of Augmented Reality

Boo-Gyum Kim[1], Jong-Soo Choi[2], and Jin-Tae Kim[3]
[1]Solutionix Co., Ltd, Seoul, Korea
[2]Department of Image Engineering, Graduate School of Advanced Imaging Science, Multimedia and Film, Chung-Ang University, Seoul, Korea
[3]Department of Aerospace Software Engineering, Hanseo University, Chungnam, Korea

Abstract –*Augmented reality is the field that provides users with more information by registering virtual objects in realistic images acquired from the camera. In this paper, an augmented reality system was implemented using the SIFT algorithm on behalf of marker recognition.*

Keywords: augmented reality, virtual object, SIFT, marker, feature points

1 Introduction

Augmented reality is the technology to implement a newer computing environment by registering virtual objects in realistic images derived from the camera and providing users with its outputs. A variety of techniques are used in augmented reality. Major techniques include 3D modeling that makes virtual objects, camera calibration to compute camera variables, the tracking algorithm that finds the location of objects, and registration that combines virtual objects with realistic images. The most general method to implement augmented reality is to use separate markers that have earlier-defined shapes and patterns. Therefore, under the conditions without markers, the implementation of augmented reality becomes highly difficult.

In this paper, aimed at implementing augmented reality, a real-time camera tracking technique that does not use separate markers is proposed. The proposed method detects ground planes on the three-dimensional space using the SIFT (Scale-Invariant Feature Transform) algorithm, and based on it, performs real-time camera tracking and the registration of virtual objects. Accordingly, this technique is capable of implementing augmented reality without separate markers that are used in existing methods such as ARtoolkit [1].

2 Extraction of Feature Points

The SIFT algorithm extracts robust size and rotation features. Feature vectors from this are characterized by the stability of image sizes and rotations. The SIFT algorithm generally goes through the following four phases.

Step 1) Scale-space extrema detection

Step 2) Key-point localization and filtering

Step 3) Orientation assignment

Step 4) Key-point descriptor

3 Proposed Algorithm

The system implemented in this paper is shown in Fig. 1.

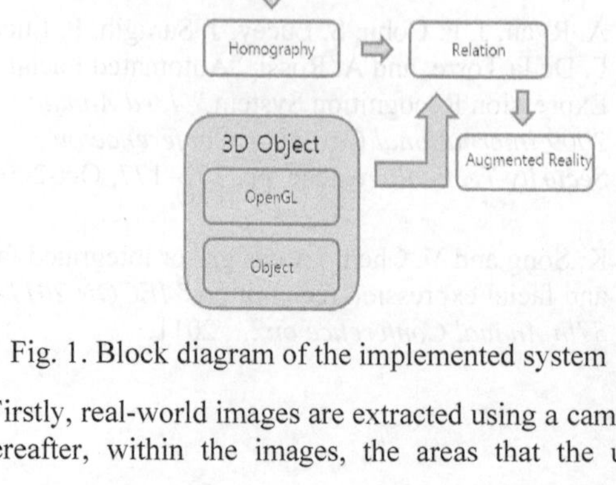

Fig. 1. Block diagram of the implemented system

Firstly, real-world images are extracted using a camera. Thereafter, within the images, the areas that the user meaningfully captured are extracted. With regard to the user images and the real-world image areas obtained in real time, the feature points of each image are extracted using the SIFT algorithm. After estimating the homography relationship regarding the extracted feature points, planes for the user images are obtained. Finally, using OpenGL, virtual objects are registered on the planes.

In order to improve the speed of the SIFT algorithm, the SIFT algorithm was applied to the obtained plane areas in a limited manner. In addition, accuracy was improved by increasing the number of feature points found in the areas and heightening matching sensitivity. The corresponding results were confirmed by a test.

4 Experiment and Discussion

A test was performed on the proposed system. Firstly, 320×240 images were extracted using the camera in an indoor environment, and then their user areas were defined. Thereafter, base on the results of extracting and matching the features of the real-time camera images and the characteristics of the user images, an augmentation test was conducted. Fig. 2 shows the testing on the accuracy of the overall system's UI and the accuracy of the camera-derived images. As shown in Fig. 3, the extraction of the feature points of the user-defined images was confirmed.

Fig. 2. UI of the overall system

Fig. 3. Extraction of feature points

Fig. 4 exhibits the matching between user-defined images and camera-derived real-time real-world images, the application of homographies and the extraction of planes.

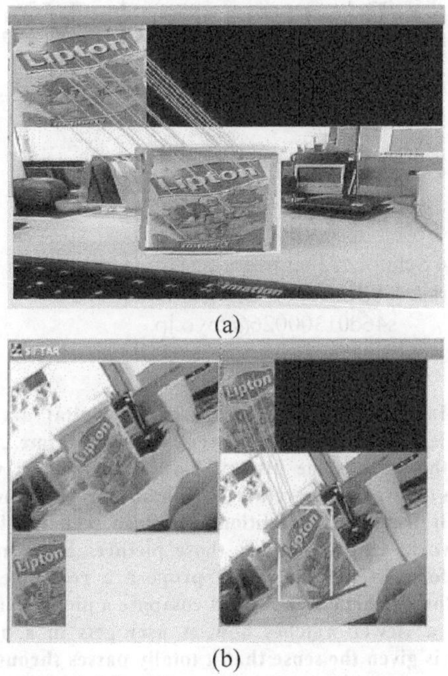

(a)

(b)

Fig. 4. Matching with real-world images

5 Conclusions

This paper proposed a system that tracks objects, implements planar homographies, and augments virtual objects on matched objects by using the extraction of features points based on the SIFT algorithm and a matching algorithm. The ARToolkit library's marker-based augmented reality is easy to use and of good performance. However, this technique not only involves the limitation of having only fixed patterns, but also cannot perform augmentation if the patterns are hidden or removed. On the other hand, because the SIFT-based augmented reality system uses natural features that do not have fixed patterns, it has the advantage of robust augmentation even when patterns are hidden. Moreover, with an additional ability to track real-world natural objects, it has the advantage of being able to compensate for the artificiality of markers.

6 References

[1] ARToolkit, http://www.hitl.washington.edu/artoolkit

[2] Ronald. T. Azuma, "A Survey of Augmented Reality," *Hughes Research Laboratories, Teleoperators and Virtual Environments*, vol. 6, pp. 355-385, Aug. 1997.

[3] David G. Lowe, "Distinctive Image Features from Scale-Invariant Keypoints," *International Journal of Computer Vision*, vol. 20, no. 2, pp. 91-110, 2004.

[4] V. Lepetit, "Point Matching as a Classification Problem for Fast and Robust Object Pose Estimation," *Computer Vision and Pattern Recognition*, vol. 2, pp. 244-250, 2004.

Proposal of the Digital Art Watching System Letting Picture and Visitor Fuse in Real Time

Koji Fujita
Graduate School of Engineering, Toyo University
Kujirai2100,Kawagoe-City,Saitama, Japan
s46d01300026@toyo.jp

Takayuki Fujimoto
Graduate School of Engineering, Toyo University
Kujirai2100,Kawagoe-City,Saitama, Japan
me@fujiotokyo.com

Abstract—**In this study, we propose the digital art view system which lets a picture and a viewer fuse in real time. As the background, the art has the history. To date much art works were shown in the world. Therefore, the picture projects the time. For example, it drew social conditions and drew scenery picture. Various art works exist. However, those pictures are plain art works. Therefore, in this study, we propose a real-time view system using the synthetic technique. I compose a picture and the viewer whom a viewer watches now. A user gets in a picture afterwards. It is given the sense that it totally passes through the frame, and seems to enter the picture to a viewer. It is a new digital art system.**

Keywords—art; ; art museum; communication;

I. INTRODUCTION

The art is the historical thing which supported by culture of the entertainment in the life of the person. The picture reflects social conditions. It affected many people who saw the picture. However, those pictures were drawn on a plane. Many art museums don't let you touch those important art works because there are the possibilities of lost or wreck of works. Visitors can look only from constant distance away because of that. We thought that the picture could see it with more interesting if visitors could touch the art works. We thought it can get author's feelings and the thought. However, it is essentially difficult to touch the art works. Therefore, we plan to use the synthetic techniques. We compose the picture and visitors by specific synthetic processing software in real time. We project a synthetic image to a monitor afterwards. From this result, visitors could feel the entertainment in the picture more. Because of this, visitors enter the frame in real time and the image was synthesizing. This becomes the digital art work which rise entertainment characteristics. The digital art system which let you such information technology and art fuse thought that there might be demand. In addition, in this paper, we propose the digital art view system which lets the picture and viewer fuse in real time.

II. PURPOSE OF STUDY

In this paper, the purpose of that is let a displayed picture fuse with information technology and makes the digital art system. In the current art museum, visitors could watch only from some distant away from displayed work of art. However, the system to propose in this paper is synthesized in real time when the visitors entered to the appointed space of the certain uniformity and look at a picture. The method synthesizes both data of picture and visitor by Chroma Key. In addition, this system compared to the figure of the visitor with the picture. This is because it displays a visitor in the picture with real size. This gives the sense that got into the picture to a visitor. In addition, this system can let a visitor feel it in real time. This system is not works for just to watch a picture. Visitors always look at pictures on a plane. However, they can look at this system for the sense that seemed to enter the picture. Furthermore, we can propose system that enable unprecedented picture viewing of visitor participation type.

III. SYSTEM SUMMARY

We will explain the summary of this system in this chapter. This system projects the image which converted an art work into data and shown to monitor. Then, the visitor who came to watch a picture watches the monitor. Take movie of user by a camera installed in the upper part of the picture afterwards. Finally, it Synthesizes a picture and a visitor in real time.

A. About space to perform Chroma key

Gallery space, which perform chroma key on carrying out this system, is necessary. Therefore, it is important to make space such as figure 1.

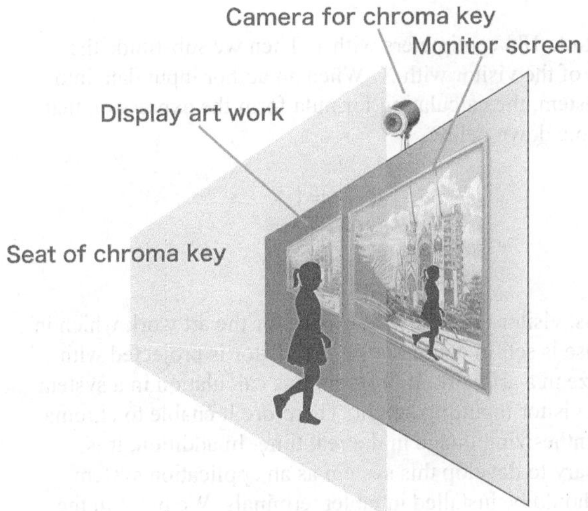

Figure 1 Environmental to perform chroma key.

It display the art work in the same way as the normal art museum. Monitor is set on the side. In addition, there is a camera to reflect visitor to the monitor. This inputs projected over the wall exhibiting art work. The visitor image converted to size in comparison with the specific object in the picture. Therefore, image height and place is not problem.
Behind the visitor, a green sheet is set. This sheet is necessary to perform Chroma key. In addition, we put a camera on the upper part of the wall of the picture in the environment. As a result, the wall which display art work set at lower place than sheet side. Because of this, the environment build the digital art system which reflected a visitor in the real time.

In this study, this system need the following machine to let a art work link the visitor in real time.

(1). Sheet for chroma key
(2). Camera for chroma key
(3). Monitor for chroma key
(4). System for input the height of the visitor

These are the necessary items.

B. Sheet for chroma key

When we take synthesized video, chroma key is used. Green background is necessary for it. For example, target person wants to make synthesis image flying into the sky. In this case, we need to make a motion that the target is flying in front of a sheet of chroma-key. It synthesize the target image and blue sky. In the result, it can create the synthesis image which there is flying in the sky. Figure 2 is an example of the studio using sheet of chroma key.

Figure 2 Example using sheet for chroma key

Thus, only visitor have to do is watching an art work and this system can synthesize an art work and visitor.

C. Camera for chroma key

Next, we will explain the camera for chroma key. We show the camera for chroma key in figure 3.

Figure 3 the camera for chroma key

This camera is handy camera of Sony HDR-PJ390. This is machine to use when we sysnthesize visitor and an art work. This camera puts on a wall displaying a art work and it take a visitor movie. Thus, it does not give discomfort for visitor watching an art work and it can watch an art work in natural form.

D. Monitor for chroma key

In this paper, a monitor always projecting the art work image. It projects the picture of chroma key made in the realtime when visitor came in front of the art work. We show a monitor to use in figure 4.

Figure 4 Figure of monitor for chroma key

The monitor of figure 4 is liquid crystal display LB-T401 of the SHARP40V type for business use. The monitor will chose the size that would be equal to a picture. Therefore, we use these machine. The visitors will see one's figure watching a picture by putting this monitor on the wall. The visitor feel they enter the world of the picture when they see the monitor

E. System to input the height of the visitor

This system synthesize a visitor and an art work. Accordingly, this system compare the shape of the art work which it set with the height of the user. Therefore, this system synthesize it based on the shape that it calculated. This system project the result to a monitor. Thus, a system, to input the height of the visitor, is necessary. We show input system in figure 5.

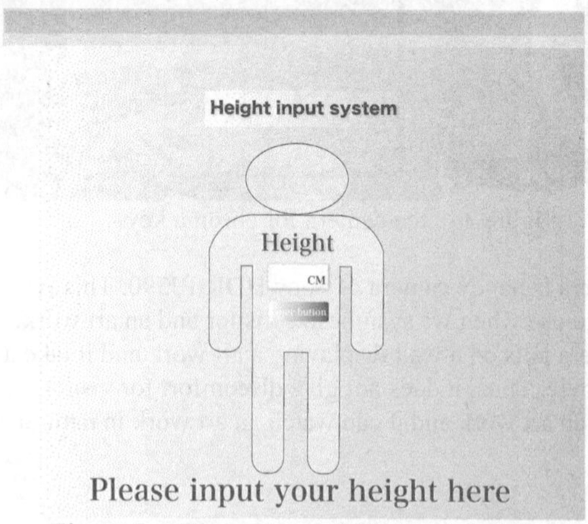

Figure 5 The system which inputs height

This system is to input the height of a visitor who watching an art work. Visitor input height into this square frame. It calculates an art work shape and the ratio of the visitor , then it make real size when we compared the visitor with the art work. For example, when author use this system. Height of author is 174 centimeters. Thus, author inputs the height in a square. When input is completed, user push the decision button under the input box. The data of the height which a visitor who are watching a picture, are sent. For example, it assume that there is the art work which it drew a person image on. Let we say the height of the drawn person is 180 centimeters. we substitude 180 centimeters with 1. Then we substitude the height of the visitor with X. When an author input data into this system, the calculating formula form the expression that we wrote down below.

$$180:174=1:X$$
$$180X=174$$
$$X=0.966\ldots$$

Thus, visitor is about 96% of size for the art work which in this case is set. In consequence,the visitor is projected with real size in a art work. It program this calculation in a system which visitor inputting height. Therefore,it enable to chroma key synthesizing image in the real time. In addition, it is necessary to develop this system as an application system. This should be installed in tablet terminals. We put it in the place where a picture is displayed. In consequence, a visitor does not have to carry a device.

Ⅳ. PROPOSAL SYSTEM

We used the software which perform chroma key to suggesting this system by "Institute for system plan Co., Ltd., ISP." This system is called "ROBUSKEY LIVE." As for this software, there is best matche computer is selling together. We use this computer and software to realize synthesis image real time. We show a computer to use in figure 6.

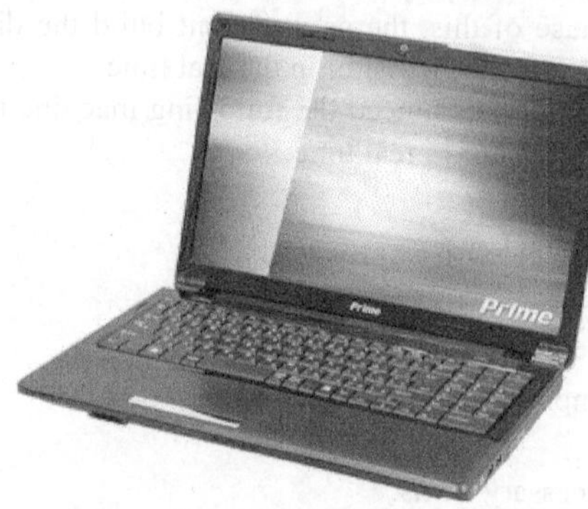

Figure 6 The computer which was equipped with "ROBUSKEY LIVE"

This software perform chroma key. At first, it take by using camera. It is perform that it synthesize background image which we set to the computer and taken information. For this reason, the digital art system in this study is possible. Here, we show the flow of the system in figure 7.

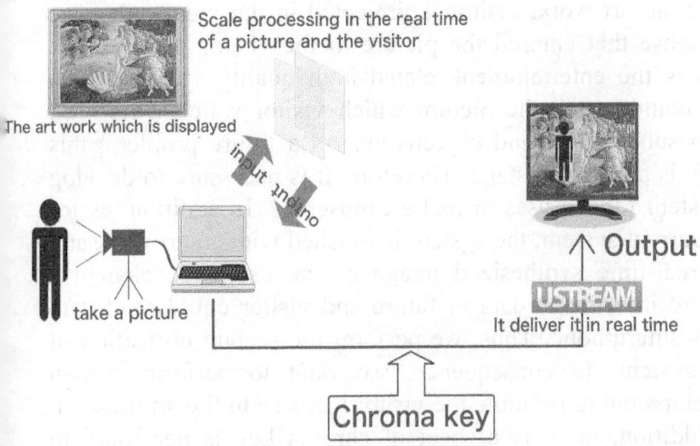

Figure 7 Flow of the system

First of all, it takes a visitor who watching an art work in front of a sheet for chroma key. 「ROBUSKEY LIVE」 Secondly, there is a computer equipped with "ROBUSKEY LIVE" and user choose the background image letting you synthesize it here. Thirdly, the picture of the visitor which took using a camera is performed chroma key. Next, we broadcast this picture to USTEREAM. It performs the broadcast of this USTEREAM by limited account. Thereby, it prevent it from leaking picture outside. Then, it acquire a picture broadcast to USTREAM with other computers. We connect the computer and monitor using an HDMI terminal. Finally, it projected picture to a monitor. By the flow of these system, we can propose the digital art system in the real time. Furthermore, the visitor input one's height into the system before reflecting visitor in art work. Therefore, visitor is synthesized with real size in it. We explain an object to compare. The used art work really sets one any object. It compare the value of the visitor with the value and it is synthesize afterwards.

Then, we give the example using the system. I explain this using a real art work. It assumed that an author used a system. We perform it with the art work of "the Henry VIII image" which Hans Holbein drew. I show the picture in figure 8.

Figure 8 Henry VIII image

It is said that Henry VIII was about 190 centimeters. Accordingly, I set the subject of this picture with 190 centimeters. For example, an author uses it in this system. Height of the author is 174 centimeters. We show a figure after having done chroma key in figure 9.

Figure 9 Picture at the time of the system use

We consider the case that I used chroma key and watch an art work as digital art this time. It was able to do a comparison between one's height and Henry VIII's height. This cause author watch a picture subjectively more than before. I try to read a synthesized figure. It understand that Henry VIII was very big. Visitor could not feel this only by having watched an art work. In addition, you could not touch the picture. However, visitor watching picture by this system can perform action to Henry VIII . This grants the desire of the visitor. This raises entertainment characteristics of the art work.

Then, we show an example in the landscape. Here, I take up one in " Thirty-six Views of Mount Fuji" of Hokusai Katsushika. The name of the art work is "The Great Wave off Kanagawa". This is the famous picture which Hokusai Katsushika left as a woodcut. We show the picture in figure 10.

Figure 10 Picture of "The Great Wave off Kanagawa"

In the case of this picture, it is different from the picture of "the Henry VIII image". Ship, angry waves, and Mount Fuji are drawn. This is a landscape. Therefore, the real size of a visitor projected by a monitor become really small. This picture made a set point a ship. This ship is a small ship. Full length was about 12 meters. Width was about 2.5 meters. It is said that depth was about 0.9 meters. Therefore, we had a value to set the depth of the ship this time. We compare the value with the height of a visitor watching an art work. We show a figure when I used this system in figure 11.

Figure 11 The figure which was synthesized when I used this system.

We show the image which extended figure 11.

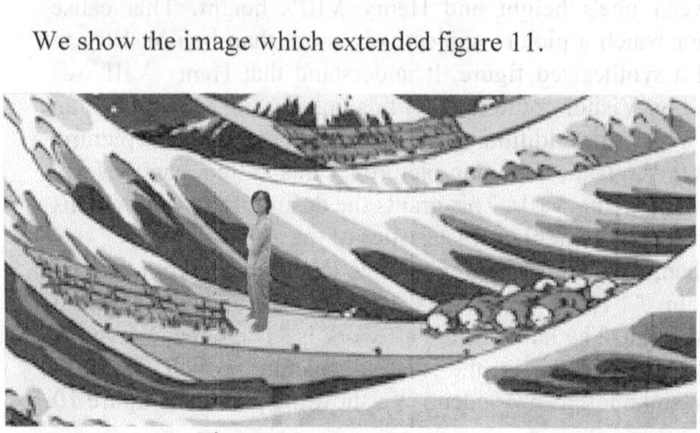

Figure 12 Extended image

I set the ship in this picture with 90 centimeters. The high wave understands well that it watch this. For this reason,the visitor watching a picture can really feel the sense that this painting contained. In the result, we were able to suggest a system as digital art by this system.

V. conclusion and consideration

In this paper, we propose the digital art watching system letting picture and visitor fuse in real time. It was important whether the art museum displayed the art work which was better than other art museums so far. However, there is different characteristic by the digital art with this system. When a visitor watches a picture, we perform it. If visitor watch an art work, visitor is projected in the picture. It gave the sense that entered the picture to the visitor who looked. This is the entertainment-related high quality system which you could watch the picture which visitor watched only on plain subjectively and objectively. As a future problem, this study is a proposal stage. Therefore, it is necessary to develop a system for the uses in real art museums. In addition, as for the current system, the system is finished with an art work and the real-time synthesized image of the user. We change a picture into image data in future and visitor could send it to one's smartphone. Thus, we perform the second utilization of the system. In consequence, we want to perform system development to promote the visitor increase to the art museum. In addition, there is a sheet of chroma key is necessary to perform synthesize. Under the present conditions, we limit space and uses of system. However, we put sheet of chroma key in all of art museums. As a result, we can perform chroma key at all places in an art museum. We put a system in each pictur. Thus, all space becomes the space that the system is available. We make come the real art museum cooperate in future true. It can be added more value to watching a picture. We want to increase visitor by this system. Finally, we perform survey with entertainment characteristics and the visibility as the digital art system after developed a system. I complete this system from the result.

References

[1] Seiki Inoue, Nobuyuki Yagi, Hideki Sumiyoshi, practice CG, picture composition to learn by C language, Ohmsha ,2005,04

[2] Sony Corporation ,http://www.sony.co.jp

[3] Sharp Corporation, http://www.sharp.co.jp

[4] Institute for system plan /ISP, http://www.isp.co.jp/products/robuskey-live/index.html Co., Ltd.

[5] Akihiro Sashi, Renaissance monarch of the labyrinth – U.K. of Henry VIII, temple of the Showa era, 2012.0630

[6] Junichi Okubo, “Thirty-six Views of Mount Fuji” of Hokusai who describes it in infinite variety, Shogakukan, 2005.9

[7] Kaoru Sugita, Toshiaki Nakasu, Yasunobu Yamauchi, display guide system expanding the museum space by the association of the showpiece, Institute of Electronics, Information and Communication Engineers technology research report. MVE, multimedia, virtual environmental basic 109(466), 41-44, 2010-03-05

[8] Satoshi Ikehata, Toshihiko Yamasaki, Kiyoharu Aizawa, The Shadow Man: The interactive media art using the shadow, Institute of Electronics, Information and Communication Engineers technology research report. MVE, multimedia, virtual environmental basic 109(466), 119-124, 2010-03-05